CW00569553

about the author

Sarah Bryden-Brown lives in Sydney, Australia.
She is a journalist and editor who has written for
*The Sydney Morning Herald, The Financial Review,
Elle, Vogue* and *marie claire lifestyle*. After leaving
school she worked in event marketing and advertising
before studying English literature and journalism at
university. She worked for *The Australian* for six years
and is currently acting editor at *donna hay magazine*.
Sarah lives with her husband, Roberto, and children,
Monte and Lucy, along with numerous chickens
and guinea pigs. This is her first book.

The Lost Art of
Childhood

How to do things families have forgotten

Sarah Bryden-Brown

RANDOM HOUSE AUSTRALIA

Random House Australia Pty Ltd
20 Alfred Street, Milsons Point, NSW 2061
http://www.randomhouse.com.au

Sydney   New York   Toronto
London   Auckland   Johannesburg

First published by Random House Australia 2003

National Library of Australia
Cataloguing-in-Publication Entry

Bryden-Brown, Sarah.
The lost art of childhood.

ISBN 1 74051 240 5.

1. Family life education. 2. Child development.
3. Children. I. Title.

305.231

Cover and internal photographs by Chris Court
Cover and internal design by Vanessa Holden/ad+d pty ltd
Internal illustrations by Anna Warren
Typeset by J&M Typesetters, Victoria
Printed and bound by Tien Wah Press Pty Ltd, Singapore

10 9 8 7 6 5 4 3 2 1

'where is the *life* we have lost in the *living*

where is the *wisdom* we have lost in the *knowledge*

where is the *knowledge* we have lost in *information*'

ts eliot

contents

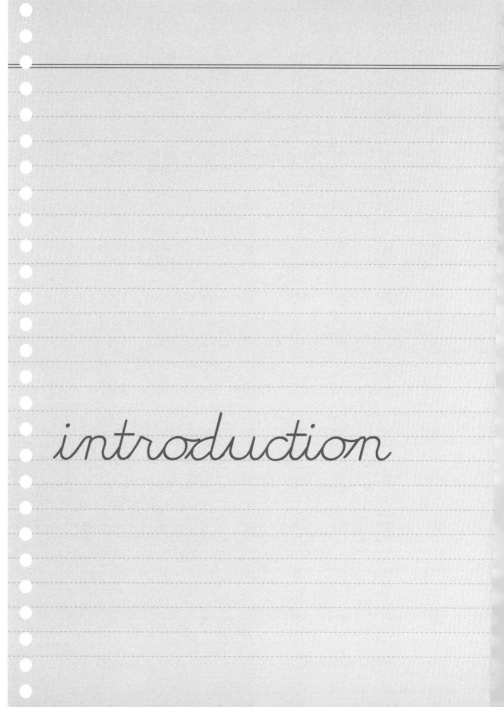

introduction

'You guys never do anything I like,' my nine-year-old son Monte
told us late one Saturday afternoon after we'd got back from seeing
a movie and Roberto had come home from a game of squash.

'What kinds of things would they be, Mont?' I asked, probably
while busying myself with something else and certainly having no
expectation his answer would change our lives.

'I want to go fishing and camping. I want to do things.'

If he had said anything other than fishing and camping we
would have probably fobbed him off with a 'Sure thing, honey' and
hoped one day to get around to whatever 'it' was or pay for him to
experience it. But the words 'fishing' and 'camping' went off like
alarm bells in our heads.

I'd always thought of our family as the archetypal modern
family, from our structure – we're a blended, two-income family –
through to our Saturdays. I first met Roberto when I was a 28-
year-old university student, part-time journalist and single parent
with a four-year-old son, Monte. We fell in love, married six
months later and by law became a family. We lived and loved day
by day with our different surnames, pursuing individual careers
and sharing hopes, failures and the housework. Three years later
our daughter Lucy came along, and life continued in our rented
house, we took out our first loan together to buy a car, opened a
joint bank account and took the kids on holidays to Daydream
Island, Byron Bay and once to America. Life was good. Everyone
was happy. It never occurred to Roberto or me there was anything
missing from our lives, until Monte turned nine and let us know

how wrong we were.

'Sorry Monte,' I said, 'I don't know the first thing about fishing or camping.'

'Me neither Mont,' added Roberto. 'How about we find a sport and recreation camp for you?'

'But I want to go with you guys.'

Well, what do you say to that?

'Looks like we are going camping,' I said.

And so, with no idea how, we took our family camping.

I can't remember having enjoyed any four days more than those spent on our inaugural camping trip to the Hunter Valley in New South Wales (NSW). It was probably the first time we had been together as a family with absolutely nothing else to distract us from enjoying the time we had with each other. It's embarrassing to say, but it was overwhelming.

And so from camping we progressed to fishing, grew an impressive vegetable garden, bought three chickens and built them a house, learnt how to knit, watched our guinea pigs have babies, and cooked together. We became a re-fashioned family.

As a journalist, I naturally became curious about why we had never before wanted to do any of these things. So I asked our friends if they had ever learnt how to fish, camp, knit, raise animals, and so on. Our friend Rachel – who has a five-year-old daughter and grew up on the NSW north coast with her two sisters and brother – told me her dad took them camping and fishing and killed their chickens regularly for Sunday night roasts.

But he taught her none of his skills because he always assumed she would marry a man who would be as clever and proficient in these things as he was. I don't know if she has told her dad yet, but Adam's not.

Other friends put our loss of these skills down to the fact that we belong to a predominantly white-collar society in which little value is attached to such things. My own parents, who divorced when I was a toddler and were both employed in white-collar industries, couldn't have been more different: my father, who died three years ago, tried to engage his two daughters in camping, home-movie making, carpentry, fixing up old cars and even caravanning, but we didn't take to any of it; my mother was a career woman who used her head more than her hands.

Is it just a coincidence that parenting today has become dominated by the need to drive our children academically, musically, theatrically, in the pool and on the sports field, at the cost of these fundamental life skills that teach more than the sum of their parts? Because quite apart from the pleasures and bonding offered by such activities, these traditional, old-fashioned treasures – knitting, fishing, and camping, to name just three – provide invaluable first-hand lessons in maths, science, geography, logic, reasoning, communication and commitment.

The things we've discovered together have also given us a great way to relax from a couple of stressful day jobs: there is nothing better than feeling physically exhausted when all you're used to is mental exhaustion. We also never imagined we would embrace

some of these activities in the way we have – camping now has a
regular spot on the calendar, I am still knitting, the chickens have
had their first birthday and I am determined to cook a fish that
has been caught by someone I am related to.

I've had a lot of fun researching this book – and a couple of
surprises, too. One is how much Roberto and I have learnt, and
how rewarding that has been, not only because we are learning
something new but because we are learning it with the kids.
Parenting is by its nature so much about teaching, that to be able
to admit you've no idea about something, and then to form a
partnership of discovery with your children, allows them a sense of
independence while also bringing you closer together.

So here's what we've learnt since Monte turned nine. I hope our
experiences will inspire you to launch your own voyage of
discovery and provide you with the basic information we gathered
on our accidental journey to the lost art of childhood.

acknowledgements

Sometimes I thought I would never be able to finish this book,
what with all the time spent camping, fishing, knitting ... but it's
an achievement underpinned by the love and immense support of
my family and friends. Without the walks around the park with
my astute friend, Lisa Hoppe, my head would have burst with all
the wondering I was doing. Without James Hall, the literary editor
of *The Australian*, I would never have had the confidence to send
my idea to a publisher. Often I called him in despair and with his
few, carefully chosen words I found the confidence to keep going;
my publisher Jane Palfreyman from Random House seamlessly
took over this supportive role with warmth and professionalism.
Without Vanessa Holden, the designer, I wouldn't have been lucky
enough to have such a beautiful-looking book and without Jane
Gleeson-White, my editor, my words would have suffered. Without
my mother-in-law, Joan, whom I love dearly, I would not have had
the unconditional support I needed to complete this book and, of
course, without my two beautiful and life-affirming children I
would never have been able to indulge in such childish behaviour.
But the greatest debt I owe is to my husband Roberto. As he once
said to me, with a smile on his face and in his heart, 'God knows I
was put on this earth to sort out your emotions.' I would only add,
'And make me what I am today.'

camping

When we walked through the huge old wooden door of Roberts, the beautiful but expensive restaurant in NSW's Hunter Valley wine district, we looked appalling. I had on thongs and a sarong I'd worn for the past four days, Roberto smelt like a camp fire and the children could easily have been mistaken for street kids. But judging by the look on each of our faces, you knew we had arrived with a mission.

A month earlier I had been washing up when Monte came in and asked if we could go camping for Easter. Camping wasn't a regular activity in our house when I was his age. Dad took us a couple of times — though pitching ourselves against the elements wasn't the motivation, rather it was a way of sleeping on his new piece of land in the middle of the bush while he prepared to build a house. I am sure we had fun, but there was never any: 'Come here Sarah and I will show you how to tie off tent ropes', or, 'This is how you build a campfire'. Camping practices weren't an integral part of Dad's fatherly repertoire. But I hadn't been put off, which is why I happily agreed to go camping with my boyfriend when I was in my late teens — and that is where my abhorrence was born and why I said no to Monte as quickly as a reflex. My boyfriend took me 'cliché camping'. It rained, we had a dud tent and nothing we needed. I hated it. As we drove home in silence (from god knows where because I have blocked it out) I vowed to myself I would never, ever do that again.

'Why can't we go camping?' Monte persisted.

'Sport and recreation camps have great stuff like that,' Roberto said as he walked into the conversation.

'But I want to go with you guys.'

Well, what do you say to that?

'Looks like we're going camping,' I said and turned to Roberto with an amused look on my face because I knew he disliked the idea as much as I did.

I spent the following week looking into where we should go — but because camping types are so well-organised there wasn't much left to choose from. While I had agreed to go camping, that didn't mean I would sleep next to a cement toilet block. I wanted seclusion, but fresh water; to be by the water, but with privacy; somewhere north, for warmth, and only a couple of hours of driving. Motherhood is not the same as martyrdom.

I presented my short list over dinner one night so everyone could have their say and Lake St Clair in the Hunter Valley was the unanimous pick. It is a couple of hours from Sydney, so it wouldn't be as crowded as the closer, more popular sites (that were already booked out anyway); it was amongst the wineries, which meant we would have something to do during the day if needed; and it was by the water so we could swim.

Roberto's oldest brother kindly lent us his camping gear that included two tents, a ground sheet, and a folding table and chairs. As this camping caper was only ever going to be a one-off, I justified buying the family sleeping bags by saying they would come in handy for lots of other things. So why did I also buy a hurricane lantern, waterproof matches, a wire toaster, and enamel plates and mugs? Because a camping store does to me what stationery and hardware stores always do: makes me think I need everything in sight.

Having squashed too much into the car we pulled out of our street, had our usual argument about needing a station wagon, and drove 20 minutes north before pulling into a service station to fill up with petrol. Stacked outside — and stamped with the logo of the service station — were bags of firewood and Roberto bought one for the open campfire we would build each night. Roughly two hours later, as the road wound its way to the top of a ridge, a giant puddle came into view.

Our apprehension eased with this glorious sight. Lake St Clair is a man-made lake created when the valley was flooded to provide Singleton and surrounding areas with water. As it's 1540 hectares we thought we would be able to find our own private spot by the calm waters of this serene scene and spend twilight with a glass of local wine, sharp cheese and vast emptiness. Now we were verging on excited and the kids strained to see out the window to pick the perfect spot for us to live for the next four days. We hurried down the other side of the mountain and turned into the entrance.

Bumping along in our city car we tentatively drove over grassy hills looking for our special spot. While the view from the ridge was expansive, the Lake St Clair camping ground was contained.

After doing a two-minute loop, a couple of times, we wondered why everyone was camping as if they were sharing the same tent pegs. Either the squashed campers knew something we didn't or their reason for camping was the antithesis of ours. Feeling intimidated by their collective strength of camping paraphernalia we headed for the top of the hill, as close to the privacy of the perimeter fence as possible. Looking out across the lake we liked what we saw, so extricated ourselves from the car and took in the moment. Down there were the professionals. Everyone had trailers and every one of those trailers was full of tree trunks and branches. Up here we had no idea what we were doing and a bag full of suburban service station wood.

After re-pitching both our tents away from the ants' nests we unfortunately disturbed, we set up what was to be our rural retreat. As early as the first night, when Roberto and I were getting dinner ready, I started to fall in love with camping. Having taken Monte to help fill up the boot with dead tree branches, Roberto was now in the process of building a fire so we could cook sausages. I was pouring two glasses of wine and preparing to light the lantern for when it got dark. The kids were running — everywhere. They had Lucy's plastic ball and were laughing their heads off as she tried her hardest to do running kicks. All I could think of was: they call this 'the witching hour' back home.

All the sausages rolled off the griddle plate and fell onto the grass just as I reached the table. But as we were already laughing while arguing over how to light the lantern, it only made us laugh harder. So we dusted them off and ate every one, along with our fresh ears of corn boiled in the billy, and a buttered loaf. It was now 7.30 pm, the kids had washed up in Lucy's old nappy bucket, and we had nothing to do and nothing to distract us from doing nothing. Lucy was excited about going to sleep in a tent and couldn't wait to crawl into her sleeping bag in between ours. Roberto and I read her a story each as Monte indulged his pyromaniac fantasies. But as we went to crawl out she became scared of being in there all by herself.

'Listen for our voices, Luce,' I told her. 'We are sitting right outside and you will be able to hear us talking all the way to sleep.'

As we lulled her to sleep with our arguing over the rules to gin rummy, we made our first pot of billy tea. We knew you had to swing the can around using the full circle of your arm, but no one was game to try because one moment of timidity can cause third degree burns. So we tapped it with a stick instead and drank in the only kind of solitude that can exist when three people are sitting under a canopy of stars on a warm, clear night after a day replete with laughter, food and those you love the most.

Our days at Lake St Clair were spent either touring the local vineyards or hanging out at the campsite. They also began awfully early. Considering we needed to make a fire, collect water to boil for washing up, cook breakfast, wash up and ensure all our food was safely stored away, it was amazing that we were always ready for the day by 7 am. How come we can't do this at home? I wondered aloud each morning. I read recently that the Easter weekend is notorious for wet weather, though 2000 and 2001 were exceptions. We were the lucky recipients of 2001's glorious sunshine, which meant Roberto and the kids could swim in the lake each day. I didn't because it had a yucky weedy muddy bottom. Sometimes in the afternoon we went for a swim in the local pool after collecting home-grown vegetables from roadside stalls. We weren't apart for a minute of those four days and I loved every one of them. There is nothing like relying on one another, as we did, and there were only a couple of grumbles from the kids about the jobs they had to do.

Monte's pet hate was collecting fresh water each morning. To punish us for making him do such a difficult, trying, awful task he took his time, exaggerating the struggle. Lucy's was washing up, but here we had the opposite problem. Once she started she never wanted to finish and would diligently wash everything twice or sometimes three times as we all complained about wanting to get going so we could go swimming. Perhaps if the weather wasn't so beautiful our inauguration would have been different, but it was more than just the weather that made those four days one of the best holidays we have ever had. It was the mixture of challenges, relaxation and discovery — but most of all it was because we were doing it all together.

Which is why, I guess, everybody else at Lake St Clair was camping on top of one another. Perhaps they are whole streets of families who share their holidays as well as daily life. The kind of camping we did wasn't what you would call 'remote'. We weren't more than 20 minutes from a town and there were freshwater tanks at the site. But that didn't mean we didn't want to peg out our own private space.

Our last morning arrived and we sat with steaming cups of billy tea and a breakfast made from canned whatever-was-left while discussing what we should do as the site had to be vacated by lunchtime. (The ranger had come around on the first day to collect our fees for the four days — $12.50 for up to four people per night — and explain how the camping ground worked.) We were in the midst of salivating over what we could have for dinner once we were home, having eaten frugally these past four days, when I suggested we stop at Roberts on the way home.

'What's Roberts?,' asked Monte.

'It's the most amazing restaurant in an old convent building with soaring ceilings and the most divine food. There are tables outside on the wraparound verandah that is covered with climbing roses, which look out over rows of grapevines. And they make the best chips.'

Our only hesitation was whether they would let us in. Dishevelled didn't cover it — we looked dreadful. But the anticipation of a three-hour lunch at Roberts gave us the courage to try. We pulled into the gravel drive and, definitely intimidated, made our way to the entrance. Just as we were about to explain our state we were offered a table for four. Accepting a couple of baby Easter eggs as we followed the waiter, we watched ourselves being watched as we walked past crisp linen shirts, neat ties and plenty of hair product before arriving at our table on the wraparound verandah that is covered with climbing roses, which looks out over rows of grapevines.

Like I said before, motherhood is not the same as martyrdom, and sitting with my family in this luxurious setting, watching their same beatific expression, was the perfect ending to four wonderful days. I now love camping — but I also love lunches at Roberts. Juxtapose the two and the best of each is magnified.

Driving home we started to plan our next camping expedition — well, the kids and I did because we're planners; Roberto is spontaneous, if there aren't any manuals or instructions to pore over. Lots of suggestions were thrown around and we finally settled on finding a location by the beach, which we all love. Fired up by the fabulous time we had just enjoyed we were full of motivation, but what would happen once we got back into our routine at home? Too often we talk about doing things but don't get around to making them happen. Time runs away, too much is happening, someone has work to finish. But I wanted to experience what we just had again, a lot.

It took a year until we finally found a week to squash too much into the car, argue over it not being a station wagon, and pull out of our street. Except this time we didn't buy service station wood because we knew better than that — we were experienced campers.

Treachery Beach at Seal Rocks was our destination, four hours

9

north of Sydney. This time Monte took a friend and both were looking forward to a week's surfing at Treachery, or Heaven, if you're a surfer. We'd also added fishing to our repertoire by that stage, so rods were tucked in amongst surfboards and secured to the roof racks.

I don't think there is a more exquisite location than Seal Rocks on the north coast of Australia. And that's not just because it is beautiful, unspoilt and offers the opportunity for luxury or roughing it. It's because it is like a mini tropical island, Australian-style. Its only access is a dirt road — which our city car was more than capable of navigating — before dividing to Seal Rocks and Treachery Beach. Seal Rocks is a flat beach with deep blue sparkling translucent water surrounded by rugged rock formations nestling small splashing pools. It has a general store and a mixture of weatherboard and luxury homes dotted along its crescent-shaped coastline. There are also small wooden cabins for hire just a couple of metres from the sand. But if surf is your thing, then follow the dirt road off to the right and you will arrive at Treachery Beach camping ground. It is hidden in bushland behind a skyscraper sand dune. This is where we were going.

With some experience under our belts we had packed a couple of tricks of the trade. I had made a curry before leaving home, frozen it, and placed it in a cooler bag for the car trip. Roberto and I enjoyed it for dinner the first night while the kids ate spaghetti bolognaise. Now I know this is not what you would call 'roughing it', but I don't want to rough it. I want the experience of sleeping under the stars with a belly full of homemade hot curry washed down with a couple of cold beers.

The boys cleverly pitched their two-person tent while we put ours up in just minutes, quite different from a year ago. We had since bought Monte a stretcher bed, so saved a lot of time in pumping up airbeds, and he assembled it himself, too. But we still hadn't committed to camping enough to have bought our own tents; they were on loan again.

At first light the next morning we were scaling the sand dune to spend the day playing on the 3 km beach along with perhaps ten other people. The vastness was intoxicating while the waves showed no mercy. Lucy didn't swim at this beach, nor did I. Despite having spent most of my holidays as a kid at a surf beach I don't like the waves. For me swimming is all about lying back and letting go, not worrying that something is about to knock you off your feet and fill your swimmers with sand. So we alternated between the two beaches — treacherous Treachery and smooth Seal Rocks. We made sand castles and watched Monte and his mate surf Treachery in the morning before returning to camp for lunch. Each afternoon was spent at Seal Rocks, fishing and swimming in its blue lagoon.

With not as much room to spread out as at Lake St Clair, we weren't close enough to share tent pegs, but were close enough to say hello to our neighbours each morning. And true to Australian tradition, the kids made friends and went to next-door's fire for dinner on the last night.

Sweeping out the tent on the final morning with the dustpan and brush I had brought along (something else I learnt from Lake St Clair: it is so much easier to sweep out your tent with a dustpan and brush than with your hands) I thought about Roberts. Crawling backwards out of our tent I said to Roberto, 'Let's find somewhere for lunch on the way home.'

If Roberts was all about the environment — stunning wineries with food to match — then the same should apply to Seal Rocks, we thought. So Roberto and I packed up, argued with the kids about helping instead of playing on the sand dune, and with seawater hair, sandy feet and a little sunburn we headed for the only place you could possibly choose for lunch — the local surf club.

It was your traditional small town local. With carpet designed for disaster — lots of colours so a few more wouldn't make a difference — the bar and poker machines were down one end and the vinyl chairs and laminex tables up the other. Again we spent hours talking about how much fun we'd had, how many hooks and sinkers we had lost fishing off the rocks and how I couldn't wait to wash my hair that was threatening to become dreadlocks. This while we were stuffing ourselves with prawn cocktails, a seafood platter and too many hot chips — there was no way we weren't visiting the dessert trolley with its homemade pavlova, chocolate mousse and cheesecake. It was the best food I had tasted in a long time.

good camping ideas

weather It's important to research weather patterns for areas you are unfamiliar with and the best advice can be gained from the park rangers or tourist bureaus.

ready to go Have a camping backpack ready to go to make packing for camping easier. Include a cutlery set; dinner plates and bowls; cups and mugs; a flashlight with new batteries; a first aid kit; a couple of packets of waterproof matches; and a swiss army knife. After each camping trip wash and clean the contents and repack the bag ready for the next trip.

second hand gear Garage sales and country fairs are great places for picking up second-hand camping gear.

test before you go Don't wait until you are in the middle of nowhere before you realise your lantern doesn't work, you're missing all the tent pegs or that you have a hole in your airbed. Always thoroughly test your equipment before you leave home.

wire toaster Wire toasters are available in most camping stores and cost very little. To use one effectively, the wire mesh needs to be underneath near the heat and the toast rack on top. Place it over a low flame, or coals, so the wire just turns red. If flames don't come through the wire mesh, your bread should toast beautifully.

stretcher bed **Stretcher beds are great for kids and save having to blow up numerous air beds. They cost little and pack away neatly into a small bag that is easily carried. They also make great beds for sleep-overs at home.**

camping list **Keep a list of what you need to take at home and update it after each camping trip, as it is the kind of activity where experience counts for a lot. If you refer to your list when packing you won't forget a thing.**

protecting food and rubbish **You can hang a food safe such as a hessian bag or large string bag from the branches of a tree to stop animals getting at it. This should also be done with rubbish bags. If you leave them on the ground they will certainly be torn apart by the next morning. Alternatively, store perishable food not kept in an esky in your car overnight.**

drying towels **If you can find a strong branch lying around that has lots of short branches still attached, hang it from a tree to air wet towels. Tie a piece of rope around the top of the branch and dangle it from a tree so the short branches reach upwards.**

fire starters **Collect candle stubs at home to take camping because these make perfect fire starters. Just light and place in the fire under the tinder.**

cooking fish **If you are going to fry fish in a pan, line it with aluminium foil first, to save washing up while also preventing lingering fishy smells.**

equipment

tents These range from simple two-person models to huge six-person palaces for the whole family. They are available from camping stores or you can buy one second-hand by looking through newspapers or visiting an internet auction site such as ebay. The materials a casual car camper requires aren't as high-tech as those used for hiking or specialist tents, so they're heavier. Prices range from $50 to over $1000, with an average tent that can sleep four costing between $300 and $400.

If you are camping with children it is worth investing in a smaller two-person tent for older kids and a fly is a must. It's a canopy that sits over the main tent, keeping it dry from dew, rain and anything else that is wet. You can choose between nylon or polyester as both materials are used by the top brands. The most important factor is that your fly is made from high-grade materials so you stay warm and dry.

* A tent's size is described using internal dimensions, usually shown as 'length x width x height', in centimetres.
* Manufacturers list the weight of a tent but if you are car camping, rather than hiking, size is more important than weight when choosing which tent is right for you.
* A vestibule is a fully enclosed canopy or storage area outside the main tent. Vestibules are designed for storing excess gear such as shoes and packs. However, this is an optional extra.

CARING FOR YOUR TENT

* First clear any sharp objects from the ground where you plan to pitch your tent and always use a groundsheet.

* Never pitch your tent directly under a tree as dead wood or branches could fall and rip your tent. Also, a tree will drip long after it stops raining and birds will soil your tent.

* Don't pitch your tent on perfectly flat ground as it could flood if there is a storm. Choose slightly rising ground.

* Be gentle with the zips and they will last a lot longer.

* Avoid wearing boots or shoes inside the tent. Not only will it last longer and smell nicer, it will stay cleaner.

* Keep your tent clean. Once you have finished camping, sweep out the inside of the tent with a dustpan and broom. If the outside is muddy, rinse it off and allow to dry before storing. A well-kept tent lasts.

* If it is raining when you are packing up, go ahead and put your tent away but make sure you unpack it as soon as possible once you are home to allow it to fully dry out. Never leave a wet tent packed away for more than two or three days. If the weather is still wet once you are home, pitch your tent in the rain to let the air in otherwise it will adopt a mouldy odour that is hard to shake.

* Once dry and packed away, store your tent in a dry area of the house. Garages or sheds that are prone to dampness should not be used to store tents, sleeping bags or other gear. They can go mouldy and deteriorate.

sleeping bags Before buying a sleeping bag, think about how much you'll use it and how much money you have to spend. There are three types to choose from: 100 per cent down, down/feather mix and synthetic.

	PLUSES	MINUSES
100 PER CENT DOWN	* best warmth to weight ratio * rolls into a small package * breathes best * stays warm twice as long as synthetic * can be refilled to regain its original warmth	* most expensive * useless if wet * takes days to dry out
DOWN/FEATHER MIX	* good warmth to weight ratio * rolls into a small package * breathes better than synthetic * stays warm longer than synthetic * cheaper than 100 per cent down	* expensive * useless if wet * takes days to dry out * warmth to weight ratio not as good as 100 per cent down
SYNTHETIC	* reasonably inexpensive * warm when wet	* bulky * doesn't breathe well * loses its warmth quickly

17

Once you decide what weather conditions you want to use your bag for, the season rating of the bag becomes important. Some manufacturers use a temperature rating instead but this is an optimistic figure and can vary from person to person by up to 10°C (50°F).

how to pick a campsite

WELL-DRAINED GROUND Pitch your tent on a level part of a gentle slope, preferably on grass but never clay, which will turn to mud if it rains. If there isn't any grass, but soft leaves and bracken, don't clear them away as it will also turn to mud. A rock wall, or thick bushes or trees provide a natural windbreak that you can use to shelter your tent from strong wind and rain. Pick a place where the breeze can reach you because everything will dry out a lot faster after it rains.

FAVOURABLE EXPOSURE Consider the direction of the weather (in Australia, cold fronts always arrive from the south-southwest). It's best to face your tent northeast to get maximum sun in the morning. If you are near a tree you will also have shade in the afternoon. Facing a northeasterly direction provides better protection against strong winds. It also makes it easier to light a fire or stove.

SAFE SURROUNDINGS Don't camp directly under trees because branches can fall on your tent if there is a strong wind. Avoid tall grass, who knows what is crawling through it, and swamps as you will be eaten by mosquitoes. Stay well back from the water's edge, remember tides rise, and if it is drought season, stay out of dry bushland as fire can sweep through without a minute's notice.

PURE WATER Ask whether the camping area has a pure water source close by. If it doesn't you will need to bring plenty.

AMPLE WOOD SUPPLY You need wood to build a campfire, and what is camping without a campfire? So check if there is plenty of wood available at the camping site otherwise stop at a service station on the way.

how to make a camp fire

For a fire to burn, three things are required: fuel, heat and air. It's best to build your fire on rocks, gravel or sand as these won't burn. Clear plenty of space around your fire and mark it with rocks so children know not to go too close. Bark from a dead tree, dry weed stalks and tiny twigs from evergreen trees can be collected and used as tinder for your fire.

You can break dead branches off trees or collect them from the ground to use for fuel.

Candle stubs are perfect for rainy day fire-lighting when the trees and twigs are too damp.

To make a small fire for boiling a billy for tea, lay a stick across two other sticks or two stones to make the letter H. Place the tinder under the fire stick (the horizontal one) and on top lay lots of thin

19

sticks and a couple of bigger sticks. Light your match, or place your candle stub in the tinder. Always throw your match into the fire so you can never start a fire where you don't mean to. For a larger fire, follow the same procedure except use bigger sticks and more tinder. You can put a triangle of large stones around it to support your billy.

Once you have finished with your fire, douse it with water and ensure all the embers have died. Stir the wet mass to make sure.

Never light a fire on a beach and just cover it with sand to put it out. The fire will have gone out but the embers can stay burning hot for a day or two, depending on how big the fire was. If people are walking on the beach and step on the sand where your fire was, they will be badly burnt. Always thoroughly douse a fire with plenty of water.

how to cook using a camp fire

Choose a spot on the side of the ridge that faces away from the wind for your fire. This provides a reasonable shelter from which to cook on your portable stove. Never cook inside the vestibule or tent. Carbon monoxide poisoning is a real danger, not to mention your tent catching on fire.

A campsite with plenty of rocks means you can make a fireplace by lining up two rows of even-sized rocks close enough together for your pots and pans to rest on them, and build the fire in between. For a single pot meal, make a triangle from three rocks of even size and build the fire in the middle.

The trick to cooking on a camp fire is to have the fire ready for the job you need to do — a leaping flame fire is perfect for boiling water while glowing embers are better for frying or grilling. You can determine the correct temperature by counting the seconds while holding your palm in front of the fire: hold your palm where you think the food is going to sit above the fire (obviously don't put your hand in the fire) and count (one-and-one, two-and-two etc) how long your hand can stay near the heat to determine whether your fire is:

LOW	6 to 8 counts	**120°C – 160°C (250°F – 325°F)**
MEDIUM	4 to 5 counts	**160°C – 200°C (325°F – 400°F)**
HOT	2 to 3 counts	**200°C – 250°C (400°F – 500°F)**
VERY HOT	1 count	**over 250°C (500°F)**

If you want to enjoy a cup of tea after dinner, place three small stones inside your billy and half fill with water so you can sit another small pot inside to heat or boil food.

Potatoes, corn on the cob, peas, beans and fish may be securely wrapped in individual foil parcels with a tablespoon of butter and placed directly on top of the coals. Each will take:

* corn 6 – 10 minutes,
* whole potatoes 45 minutes – 1 hour,
* sliced potatoes 10 – 15 minutes,
* fresh peas and beans 3 – 4 minutes,
* a whole fish around 20 minutes and fillets 10 – 15 minutes.

damper This bread made without yeast is traditionally cooked in the coals of a camp fire.

2 cups self-raising flour

½ teaspoon salt

1½ cups milk or water

Sift the salt and self-raising flour together (you could do this before you leave home and place in a ziplock bag). Slowly add the milk or water, mixing, until a soft dough forms. Make sure it is not too sticky or wet.

Shape the dough into a round and wrap it in baking paper, then a double layer of greased foil. Carefully place in the hot coals of the camp fire. In a medium fire, cook it for around 30 minutes; in a hot fire, 20 – 25 minutes. Serve immediately with lots of butter or golden syrup and a hot cup of billy tea.

saltwater potatoes A clever trick for making salty potatoes and corn is to boil them in a billy filled with sea water. As the billy boils the sea salt will stick to the sides and encrust your corn and potatoes. Once cooked, brush off most of the salt and your vegetables will be left with a mild salty taste.

chocolate bananas Slit the skin of a banana, cutting into the flesh, and push pieces of dark chocolate inside. Wrap the banana first in baking paper and then with a double layer of foil. Bake in hot coals for 5 – 8 minutes. Unwrap the bananas and serve immediately.

billy tea To follow the traditional method, take the billy with its boiling water out of the fire and add a teaspoon of tea for each person. Leave it to brew to your preferred strength then swing the billy round and round using the full circle of your arm. The centrifugal force settles the tea leaves at the bottom of the billy, allowing you to pour strained tea. Don't be timid when doing this or you will certainly burn yourself with boiling hot tea. Or you can tap the sides of the billy with a stick instead.

What you need to take for comfortable, non-remote car camping:

* a waterproof tent, poles and pegs
* groundsheet
* hammer for securing tent pegs into the ground
* fuel stove, fuel supply and waterproof matches
* bags for rubbish and storage
* sufficient non-perishable food and water
* cooking utensils: a frying pan and two billies (make sure one can fit inside the other so you can use it as a double cooker), long barbecue tongs, spatula and a good cooking knife
* cast iron plate or frypan for cooking over an open fire
* plastic colander for draining pasta, vegetables
* plastic wrap, ziplock bags, aluminium foil and paper towels
* plastic or enamel dinner plates, bowls, mugs and cups
* air beds, stretcher beds or sleeping mats and a foot pump

23

* sleeping bags, liners and pillows (liners save having to dryclean your sleeping bags regularly)
* comfortable clothing and covered shoes or boots
* swimming costumes
* raincoat
* hat and sunscreen
* insect repellent
* well-stocked first aid kit
* camera and film, binoculars if you have them
* torch, gas lantern and fuel
* esky
* table and chairs (if there is anything worth investing in it should be this: it makes a huge difference if you have somewhere to sit and eat)
* toilet paper
* washing-up detergent and two tea towels
* dustpan and broom
* bath and/or beach towels
* corkscrew, bottle opener and can opener
* swiss army knife
* bucket with a lid
* nylon rope

fishing

Monte wants a fishing rod for his birthday. This is so unexpected I decide it's because he has been watching too much television, too many cheesy American family hours. Surely there is a catch — perhaps he is hatching a plan. He asks for a fishing rod and I gush over him for his simple tastes and unsophisticated interests in the age of the computer, then reward such wholesome behaviour by buying the latest computer game. But he really does want a fishing rod and I am in trouble — I don't know how to fish and I don't want to.

My mother-in-law, Joan, calls a few days later to ask what Monte would like for his tenth birthday. I tell her he has asked for a fishing rod. She likes that idea, mainly because she knows what a fishing rod is. More often than not her nine grandchildren speak a whole other language when asking for presents. She always smiles and nods but looks at the corresponding parents with inquiring eyes. The corresponding parents respond with a smile and a shake of the head that means, Don't worry, I'll get it for you. But a fishing rod Granny can do.

Joan picks Lucy up from kindy once a week, so she arranges with Monte to take him to the local tackle shop after school to buy his rod. Monte is both excited and bothered by this. He keeps asking me to get it for Granny and finally I work out why: he thinks Joan will buy him a baby's fishing rod. Monte, who is going through a phase of defining himself by what he has rather than who he is — and I call it a phase because I am determined it will pass (wish me luck) — wants a rod that will make him look like he's been fishing all his life.

'Go with Granny, Mont,' I say, 'and let her know which one you want but don't go for the most expensive, OK?'

So Joan, Monte and Lucy head to the tackle shop on a Wednesday afternoon in early March and come home with a serious-looking rod and reel. Now it's over to me, because Roberto isn't keen on fishing, despite his late grandfather Lewis (Joan's father) having been an avid amateur angler who took Roberto and his three brothers fishing regularly. This could be because, without fail, Lewis would announce, 'I know this lake like the back of my hand!' — and then proceed to get everyone very lost, in the very dark wilderness.

'Let's just do it!' I say to Monte one afternoon when he calls me at work to let me know he is home safely from school, and to ask to go fishing for the 54th time. 'And don't worry that I know nothing, it will make me the perfect sidekick, because hanging out with someone really bad at fishing will make you feel really good about yourself.'

Ignoring the irony — preferring to interpret my comment as the epitome of logic — Monte agrees enthusiastically and we make a date for his first fling with Granny's gift. I should add that he agrees despite knowing my one and only reel adventure. When I was eight years old my father took his two ribbon-haired daughters camping in the wilds of Wiseman's Ferry, approximately 150 km northwest of Sydney, on one of the every-second-weekends we spent with him. He had a plot of land by a river and talked of building his dream home there (which never eventuated because fire swept through one summer, followed the next week by floods).

On this particular weekend I caught a Who-Knows-What fish which was particularly amazing considering my get-up. Dressed in a long frilly frock and platform cork sandals (my usual dress code whether I was shopping, fishing or watching television) I slipped and stumbled around on the muddy bank with a handline and hook that eventually found what it was looking for. But I refused to kill my huge fish; instead I kept it in a bucket of water, feeding it Monte Carlo biscuits until it floated to the top. My dad was really pissed with me, not so much because I had slowly tortured the fish to death, as because I wouldn't let him barbecue it.

'How can you be so mean,' I scolded, as I threw the bucket, with the dead fish still in it, into the river.

While my usual work hours are 9.30 am to 6 pm there are variations, such as 7.30 am to 4 pm or 4 pm to midnight. This particular week I am on the 7.30 am to 4 pm shift so I promise Monte we will go fishing after school (without Lucy, as Roberto is picking her up — apparently she is 'heaps small and pesky' and Monte doesn't want her to come). So armed with our buckets, filled with the world's most expensive fishing tackle, we make it down to a wharf in Sydney's Darling Point by 4.30 pm. (Roberto's father, Jim, had complemented Joan's birthday gift with a very generous $50. Takings at the local tackle shop must have soared the day Monte returned to spend his fortune, thanks to the wily shopkeeper who served him. I expected Monte to arrive home with a couple of sinkers and a few hooks, but instead he brought no change and the perfect equipment for deep-sea fishing off the coast of Portugal.)

Apart from the world's most expensive fishing tackle we also have a secret weapon, neatly folded and resting on top of our gear. Earlier in the week I searched the internet for what seemed like hours for a site that showed how to tie the sinker and hook onto a fishing line. I also hunted through a couple of bookshops during my lunch hour, but it all looked so complicated. Given that rigging your line is fundamental to fishing, you'd think that the basic instructions for it would be everywhere. Nope. I read a lot of words on fishing (and understood few) but couldn't find a simple line drawing of what I now know is a universal knot — until an old sea salt on the newspaper came to my rescue, that is. He overheard me banging on about not being able to find such information and in response he not only deposited a hand-drawn diagram on my desk, he also demonstrated the knot with some string from the stationery cupboard. Which is how we've come to be battling the winds with our hand-drawn diagram on the wharf and rigging our first line.

For safety, I should go first, I tell Monte. But he knows me too well, nods with wisdom beyond his ten years and patiently dangles his skinny little bruised legs over the side of the wharf.

'Oh my God. Look. I caught something!' With my excitement mounting I reel in a Little Something — and remember the reason I don't go fishing. There is no way I am ever taking a hook out of a fish's mouth, or killing one. So it is over to Monte and with his grubby, chewed fingers he removes that hook so deftly he looks like a pro. We don't even need to look at the measurement chart that is nailed to one of the pylons to see if my catch is big enough to keep, Mont just nudges the pinkie-sized thing back into the water.

Now it is his turn. There is hardly any testosterone coursing through his blood, yet, but with whatever he has, he flings his hook and sinker as far from the wharf as possible.

'Didn't you like how I just neatly plopped it in here?' I ask. 'Oh my God, Monte. You've caught a fish.'

But we fall silent.

'What type of fish do you think it is?' Monte asks as we watch it slowly turn red from its head to its tail. 'Maybe it's a Changing-Colour Fish,' I start to answer before realising, to my horror, that it's bleeding internally. All my motherly instincts take over.

'Quick, Monte, get that hook out.'

He's trying as fast as he can, he's wiggling it and wiggling it but it won't come out. I am on my knees willing him to work faster but can't bring myself to help. He frees the little baby stripy fish and gently plops it into the water where it floats on its side, rocking from side to side, in the rhythm of the tide.

We are silent for a bit and I feel I can't go on fishing after that. It's just too sad. So we pack up and on our way back to the car, Monte says: 'Mum, could you ask your friend in the office to take us fishing?'

Because we are meeting at 7 am we have to get up at 6 am, which makes us feel like we know what we are doing, even if we don't. Three weeks ago Monte did the maths, adding an hour for each day, to work out when high tide would hit early morning for our fishing date (high tide is the best time to go fishing because there are more fish around). Sea Salt, who is childless, was a little surprised by my request: could he take Monte and me fishing because, while we are doing OK, it would help if he could share some of those tips not found in books but passed down in families from generation to generation, except in mine and my husband's and most of our friends'.

'Like what?' he asks.

'Oh, I don't know ... how to prevent a fish from bleeding internally,' I suggest.

Sea Salt takes us to his special fishing spot where the view of the Sydney harbour bridge is sensational. But we are not here for the view, we are here for some serious fishing. Well, *they* are. Sea Salt carries everything down to the jetty in a milk crate and I think that is pretty clever — doesn't matter if everything is wet when you pack up — but it's when he unpacks it and turns it over to use as a seat that I'm really impressed. (Must steal a milk crate before next fishing trip, I think to myself as I sit cross-legged amongst old fish guts.)

Sea Salt wastes no time in catching a huge fish and Monte, who tries awfully hard to pretend he has no emotions, can't help but show admiration. I don't know if this means more to Sea Salt than he's willing to reveal but not long after he lets forth with some real insider stuff.

'The best way to catch a fish is to wait for it to bump into your hook once, then twice and on the third bump yank your line.' And then Sea Salt answers the question that has been bothering me the most. 'Don't try and take out a hook that a fish has swallowed because you will damage its gills and it won't survive. Just cut the line and throw it back. The hook will dissolve over a few days and won't cause the fish much discomfort.'

So Monte waits for the fish to bump once, twice, three times and catches plenty, one of which would break the record for the world's smallest fish. All the others are clear runners-up. Now I'm wondering if it's been a mistake to let Sea Salt get a foot on my pedestal — that is, until Lucy and Roberto arrive armed with hot chocolates, coffees and warm buns. The first thing Monte does for Lucy is catch a little fish and put it in the bucket so she can feed it. I just wish I had brought some Monte Carlo biscuits along.

The next time we all go fishing is months later, because it is one of those activities that seems to need a lot of preparation and time, I tell myself. But of course that's not the real reason I keep putting it off: it's because it is so smelly and filthy. But that's not the *real* reason either. The real reason is that I get bored just watching. I want to fish too, now.

So, during a holiday to Berry on the New South Wales south coast we drop into the local tackle shop for another bag of hooks and leave with a couple of handlines for Lucy and me. I really want ones with cork spools because I used one at Wiseman's Ferry (and in our fishpond at home) but now they sell only plastic wheels — although they do come in lots of different colours. The tackle shop guy tells us handlines are also handy for re-rigging a rod that's been snagged: so, rather than losing the line from your reel, you lose the piece of handline you've attached instead.

So we drive down to the Shoalhaven River near Berry and position ourselves on the fish-gut-covered jetty. We watch intently as Monte carefully anchors little pieces of fish fillet onto his hook and plops them into the murky, weedy water. We watch him do it again, and then we all get bored, even Monte. Lucy starts throwing whole fish into the water and Monte begins to experiment. He puts two or three bait fish onto his line in the hope of catching something really big. Roberto returns to his newspaper and I ignore them all because I am trying to catch something with my new handline.

But eventually we decide it's a dud fishing spot. You really do need to know where the action is for fishing to be even half-interesting for someone like me — and Mont and Luce. (It will never be even half-interesting for Roberto.)

At last, one summer Sunday afternoon, I finally get how easy — and fun — this fishing caper really is. The day before, after returning from the beach, Monte and Lucy both asked to go fishing. With Roberto working 24/7 at his openair cinema, I figured 'Why not?' There's nothing planned for Sunday. So I checked the newspaper and found high tide would hit at 4.30 pm the next day. Fishing would be a good way to kill the afternoon I figured, because otherwise the afternoon was likely to kill me.

I decide to make it really simple — more about *fishing* than *catching* fish — so I can relax and enjoy sitting on a jetty in Sydney Harbour with the kids. Monte packs the milk crate (that has mysteriously turned up in our chicken house) and we take Lucy's friend Giselle, from next door, and drive to the spot Sea Salt took us to. We pick up half a raw chicken fillet on the way, because bream love chicken, and we're out of the house and fishing.

We arrive before high tide hits so we can fish as it comes in. I only planned to fish for an hour but I find two hours have passed without a thought about the time. Monte and I have been having a competition — whoever catches the most fish is paid a dollar by the other.

Lucy and Giselle help us fish but get distracted by one of the fish that die after Monte takes the hook out. Unfortunately, we don't know it has died, because when Monte throws it back it swims away — or seems to. A couple of minutes later it pops back to the surface where it floats in an obviously dead way. Lucy looks like she is going to get sad (she's only three years old, but you can take her to the scariest movie and she's fine. But take her to a movie with a lost dog or alien, or a lonely dragon that has to say goodbye to its only friend in the whole world, and she'll fall apart, sobbing in the most heart-breaking way.) I think this is about to happen, but oddly enough it doesn't. Instead Lucy and Giselle take turns to lie down on the jetty and be dead fish. I see no reason to interfere — they do a very good dead fish.

At the end of our expedition, Monte and I are neck-to-neck with three fish each, all too small to keep, when we call it quits.

let's go fishing

rules and regulations Each state in Australia has different rules and regulations. In NSW everyone over 18 years of age must have a fishing licence. However, if you are fishing with children, and there is only one rod or line per child, the adult is exempt from requiring a licence. If you are caught without a licence you will be liable for a $2000 on-the-spot fine.

Fees in NSW range from $5 for three days, $10 for one month, $25 for a year and $70 for three years. Fees can be paid at tackle shops or by visiting your state's fisheries website.

Also, remember to check how many fish you are allowed to catch and the size restrictions. A lot of jetties and common fishing spots have signs showing the size of fish you can keep.

reels and rods For the beginner, choose a 10 – 12 cm (4 – 5 inches) spinning reel. If you're planning to fish from a boat or jetty, you need a rod 1.5 – 2 m (5 – 6 ½ ft) long; if your rod is for beach fishing, then go for around 2.75 m (9 ft). Do check with your tackle shop, because rod length also depends on how tall you are.

To cast, open the bail arm which controls the line and allows it to run freely from the spool, hold the line with your index finger as you grip the rod. Take the rod over your shoulder and flick it down in front of you to cast the line. Allow the line to run for as far as you need then flip the bail back into locking position. The most important lesson to learn is that a reel is not a winch, so always use your rod to bring the fish in, not the reel. You can do this by pulling back on the rod, and then winding your line in, repeating this technique until your catch is on solid ground. It helps if you think of your reel as a container for storing your line — and if you treat it this way, it will last a lot longer.

to rig your line The English call a sinker, a lead, which makes sense because its job is to weigh down your line. If you are casting into the surf, the sinker will carry your line past the waves (although not if I am casting for you) and if you are fishing in water with strong currents it will keep your bait in the same spot.

Kids tend to have trouble keeping their rods still, which gives the game away as far as the fish are concerned, but you can compensate for this by using slightly heavier line. But don't make it too heavy or they won't learn to be sensitive. Try a line with a breaking strain of around 4.5 kg (10 lb) to begin with and as they get more experienced switch to a lighter line, around 2.5 kg (5 ½ lb). If you really want to turn fishing into a sport, try a 1 – 1.5 kg

(1 – 3lb) line when catching bream, for example. You'll learn to play the fish, and catching one in this way is very rewarding — so they tell me.

If you are rigging a line for a child under eight, add a float so they can see where their line is. They may not understand what a bite feels like, but if they see the float bobbing under, they will know they have a fish.

A Number 4 hook is considered the standard size and a ball sinker is the one least likely to get caught in a snag. Depending on what you are catching, you can let your sinker run free, with a running sinker, or use a ball sinker that is secured in one spot with a knot. For the beginner, use a secured sinker.

There are many ways to rig a line depending on what you are trying to catch. I've covered the most basic rig here but if you want to learn more, you can consult more detailed books on fishing.

LINE

FLOAT

LEADER
an extra piece of line that attaches the hook, sinker and float to your line

SMALL BALL SINKER, SECURED

BAIT

get hooked A fishing hook has three parts: the shank that is the long straight bit; the bend, which forms the hook; and the barb which is the sharp point that juts from the hook.

A hook is used to hold the bait, fit inside a fish's mouth and catch the fish with the barb. A first time angler doesn't need a lot of tackle: choose three different sized hooks, three different sized sinkers and two packets of swivels (these are used to attach your hook and sinker to the fishing line). As I've mentioned, it's a good idea to buy a handline, too, because if you lose your hook and sinker to a snag then you can re-rig your line using the handline without having to cut a piece of line from your rod. (They're great for keeping younger kids and parents quiet, too.)

When you're choosing a hook, it's good to have an idea of how big the fish's mouth is you are trying catch, so you can choose a hook that will fit. You also need to know whether your intended catch has a soft mouth, such as trevally, or a tough mouth, such as a snapper. Because fish don't chew their food (they can't as they need to keep their mouth closed so they can breathe) some will crush their food as they take it and others use the teeth in their throat to grind it as it slides down. For example, tailor chop at bait and mullet suck it, so big hooks and heavy sinkers don't work well for them. A snapper, however, requires a heavy hook because its powerful jaws will easily break a light hook. With snapper and bream it's important not to use a hook that is too long or has a fine point, because it will break or bend inside their tough mouths. If you want to catch flathead, make sure you use hooks with long shanks because flathead have razor-sharp teeth and will cut through your line if given the chance.

Choose your hooks depending on what size mouth the fish you are trying to catch has. If you are not sure, small hooks are better than bigger ones. Make sure you have a lot of hooks with you, in case you get snagged and lose your hook.

If a fish swallows your hook, cut the line close to the fish's mouth and throw the fish back in. The hook will dissolve, causing the fish less distress than if you try to get it out.

If you find you are feeling nibbles but always losing your bait, it may be because you are using the wrong hook.

bait There are nearly as many types of bait available as there are fish swimming in the sea. What works on one day doesn't always work the next. Once you have picked your fishing spot, it is worthwhile investing some time in finding out what is the best bait to use. You can ask the fisheries department in the area, or check out the local tackle shop or charter operator because they will be sure to know what works.

Just like anybody, fish much prefer fresh bait to stinky stale bits. Fresh bait is easier to secure onto a hook because when bait gets old, it becomes soft and falls off with just a nudge from a hungry fish. Also, make sure you don't put too much bait on the hook, because the fish will nibble around the edges of it without swallowing the hook. Lastly, check there are no loose bits of bait hanging off the main piece.

types of bait

PRAWNS Enjoyed by bream, flathead, whiting, trevally and trumpeter. Fresh prawns are better but frozen ones are a good backup (though need to be defrosted before use and won't keep, so buy only what you need). To thread a prawn, first stick the hook into the underside, near the tail, and push it along until it comes out between the forelegs, just before the head. Keep pushing until the barbs of the hook can be seen and then pull the prawn over the barbs so only a tiny bit of the hook can be seen.

PIPIS Use for fish that like mussels and are generally caught in the surf, such as tailor, whiting, small snapper and bream. You can find them where you plan to fish by digging your feet in the sand as if you are doing the twist — pipis can hide as deep down as 15 – 30 cm (6 – 12 inches). It's best to have another kind of bait with you if you plan to use pipis because you may not always find them. If you do, pipis will keep for a long time unopened in a wet bag. They are not as popular as prawns or yabbies, though they do catch lots of different fish. To open a pipi, stick the sharp end of a knife into the muscle that holds the shell closed and twist carefully until it opens.

FISH FLESH Some fish, especially flatheads, like live bait such as yellowtail. Others such as Spanish mackerel, tailor, trumpeter and mulloway, will happily take a chunk of flesh. If you do use live bait, make sure you don't pierce the fish's backbone with your hook or it will die immediately. If you are using fish fillets, pierce the skin side first and then thread the rest of the fillet through the hook, using the point of the hook to pierce the skin each time. In this way you will offer the fish the flesh first, rather than skin, which they don't like as much.

GARDEN WORMS Fish such as bream, rock whiting, sand whiting and silver trevally happily go after a common garden worm that is still alive and threaded up the hook until the whole shank of the hook is covered. Keep worms in damp soil from your garden and they will live for weeks in a bucket.

RAW CHICKEN FILLET Keep a piece in a small freezer bag (and carefully label it so no one mistakes it for dinner) so you have ready-made bait available on call. Bream love it.

CUNJEVOI This is a sea animal that looks like a round piece of hard seaweed stuck on a rock. It has a small hole in the centre that squirts water if you push its sides. Apart from general amusement it also provides great bait. Carefully cut it from the rock and turn it over where you will find soft flesh that you can cut out and secure onto your hook.

saltwater crabs and freshwater yabbies Crabs can be caught off jetties, using bacon rind on the end of a piece of fishing line or string. Other types of raw meat can be used, but bacon rind is strong and doesn't break easily when you pull in your crab. Crabs live on food scraps on the sea bottom, so to catch them, let the bacon rind drift to the bottom. Freshwater yabbies are similar to crabs but live in creeks or rivers. To catch them you can use the same method as for catching crabs.

knots

GOOD KNOT FOR ATTACHING LINE TO SWIVEL

SIMPLE KNOT FOR JOINING TWO STRAIGHT ENDS

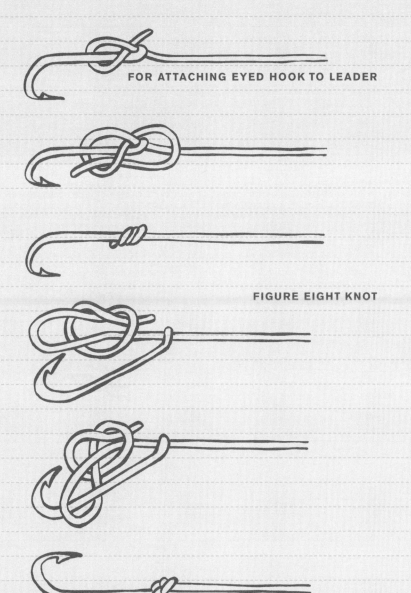

FOR ATTACHING EYED HOOK TO LEADER

FIGURE EIGHT KNOT

your fishing trip If you are new to fishing, rivers, lakes, harbours and jetties are the best places to start, because the water is calm. Remember to be very quiet because fish can hear you and any noise will scare them away.

There are two places to find fish: where they eat and where they hide. Fish normally rest in a shady place under an overhanging tree or beneath fallen logs. If they are waiting for their food to come floating along, fish will often sit behind rocks or on the tip of a sandbar.

Once you have cast your line, allow the fish to nibble your bait before you jerk your line and try to catch it. Fish need to taste the bait first, so be patient. Keep your line taut when you bring the fish in because if you let the line go slack, the bait and hook can fall out of its mouth.

There are two high tides and two low tides every 24 hours. The time of a tide moves forward by about an hour each day. Newspapers print tidal information every day or you can get a tidal chart from the fisheries department in your state. A rising tide is generally the best time to fish, though it is less important if you are going deep-sea fishing. A rising tide is important because it covers feeding grounds that have been abandoned during low tide and it also dislodges food from the sea floor, rock platforms and weed beds. If it is a particularly strong rising tide it can also unearth sandworms and clams which attract the fish.

Some fisherpeople are known to give their catch a quick kiss before releasing it back into the water. Proceed with caution.

Traditionally, fisherpeople used a creel to carry their bait and tackle to their favourite fishing spot, then used this tough cane basket to support them as they sat and waited for their catch. The creel also kept fish fresh until they arrived home with it for dinner. If you can find one, choose a creel over a plastic box because the open weave of the cane allows air to flow freely over the fish and bait, keeping it fresher for longer.

checklist

What you need to take fishing:
* a bucket with a lid
* fresh bait
* an old wooden chopping board
* hats
* sunscreen
* a fishing knife with a cover that can double as a scaler, so all the mess stays where it belongs — in the water
* a landing net (optional) — this is useful if you are catching fish that have sharp teeth, such as flathead. Rather than reel the fish in, and risk giving the fish time to bite through your line, use the landing net to scoop it out of the water
* a keep net (optional) — if you are planning on fishing for hours, your catch will stay fresher if it is kept in a secure keep net in the water.

books to read

The Old Man and The Sea *Ernest Hemingway*

This classic is the story of friendship between a young boy and an ageing fisherman, Santiago, who has to find courage in the face of defeat. Tormented by hunger and weeks of bad luck, Santiago sets out to prove his life is not finished and searches for personal triumph by travelling further out to sea than he's ever done before. For two days and two nights the old man battles a giant marlin — and himself.

Blueback *Tim Winton, Pan Macmillian, 1997, Australia*

Monte loves this book, having read it twice now, and it's a wonderful story. A young boy and his mum dive for abalone together and Abel, the young boy, makes a wonderful friend in Blueback, the groper. Of course the book has its fair share of baddies, who care little for the environment. Monte tells me it doesn't make him feel like fishing, rather it reminds him how important it is to look after the ocean and its inhabitants.

Storm Boy *Colin Thiele*

Storm Boy and his father, Hideaway Tom, live in a shack in the sandhills of the rugged South Australian coast. Storm Boy saves the life of a baby pelican and names him Mr Percival. This is the story of the strong bond that develops between them as they explore the wild and wonderful coastland.

Fishing for Beginners *Lance Wedlick, Wedneil Publications, 1985, Australia*

> This book might be out of print and a little out of date, but it is nevertheless a good overall guide for those new to fishing. You can look for it in secondhand shops.

Kids' Guide to Fishing *Mike Smith, Five Mile Press, 1991, Australia*

> Sadly this is also out of print, but it offers lots of basic information about fishing, including how to make your own keep net and landing net. You can look for it in your local library or secondhand stores.

surfing

Nearly six months pregnant with Lucy, I sat with Roberto on a deserted NSW north coast beach watching crystal cylinders roll towards the shore. As each wave broke I held my breath for the length of time it would take for my small son to be safely, albeit unceremoniously, deposited along with his Hot Grommet foam surfboard onto the sand. Being a towel-warmer from way back I knew not to comment on a failed ride, so just took a breath, smiled encouragingly and waved.

Monte will tell you he has been a surfer since he was six, which is sort of true, but he didn't get serious until around eight thanks to an inspiring lesson from a blond-haired blue-eyed Byron Bay boy who made Monte feel like a world champion. The lesson is memorable not just because Monte learnt how to surf across a wave instead of straight down it, and to lean forward to go faster and back to slow down — it's memorable because surfing really got under his skin from that day on.

When the pair finally came out of the water all pumped up they danced around the deserted NSW north coast beach describing in detail the waves Mont had caught.

'Man, that barrel was right over you, not even your Mum could see you,' said Byron Bay boy, either genuinely excited for his protégé or artificially stimulated.

But it is during a second lesson a couple of years later, for Mont's tenth birthday, that he really gets what's going on in the water. This time the lesson is in Sydney at Bondi Beach, a surfing mecca — though its surf is less forgiving than Byron Bay's neat consistency. Beholden to the tide once again, we are due to meet at 6 am. Maybe Monte would have learnt at Nippers (junior life saving lessons) what he learns this day but so far it hadn't happened because he wouldn't go to Nippers. We tried a couple of times to enrol him in what is an Australian tradition for those who live near the coast but being an impatient little thing he didn't like the queues for a two-minute paddle. He also had no appreciation for the importance of being able to read the water. Back then, anyway.

A still warm March morning on Bondi Beach changes all that. While this stocky veteran of the surf isn't as inspiring as Byron Bay boy, he does drill important information into Monte. Drawing the beach break in the sand, he points out where the rips are and how to spot them. He talks of the wind and its effect on the waves, with enough surfer-talk thrown in to keep Monte interested. He also puts an end to an argument that recycles itself in our house every few months: Why can't Monte sell his Hot Grommet, a foam board covered with material, and buy a fibreglass one? Roberto and I had come up with a bunch of reasons but none as compelling as Bondi Beach boy's. Before Monte can have a fibreglass he needs to be confident enough to swim outside the flags, he told me.

Unlike foamies, fibreglass boards are not allowed between the flags. Also, being hit by a fibreglass board hurts a lot more.

'And you know how you will learn to swim outside the flags, Mont?' we ask repeatedly. 'Go to Nippers, that's what they teach you.'

We have never been great at taking Monte surfing during winter and have only ever gone to the beach after work once, in autumn, which was a disaster. Always short for time, that early evening we tried to pack everything in. Along came the fishing rod, surfboard, fish and chips and a couple of beers. We downed the beers after a typical day at work (there should be a rule that says no one can talk until at least half an hour after adults have arrived home from work) ate fish and chips, cast the rod, snagged it and that was that.

Close to 7 pm, Monte said he was up for a surf, Lucy and Roberto went in for a swim and I sat on the sand to soak up half an hour of solitude. Two seconds later the sky went night-dark and I couldn't make out Monte from the other surfers. Terrified of swimming at night ever since *Jaws*, I stood on the shore trying to will him in. Roberto and Lucy were too far away to call in as a rescue team and I didn't want to leave the spot. What if someone surfing near him had to bring his limp little body in because of some terrible accident and I wasn't waiting for him? So I just stood there in the pitch black wondering why Roberto was still swimming with Lucy, why Monte was surfing in the dark, why I was the only one worried, why ... It was so black I didn't even see him saunter out of the surf until I felt the water spray from his shaking head. I gave him such a big hug that he looked at me suspiciously.

The same feeling of fearfulness arose during a surfing safari/camping expedition to Treachery Beach at Seal Rocks on the NSW north coast some weeks later. Renowned for its waves, Treachery is a mecca for board riders but it is not patrolled and has an oversupply of rips. Watching the local kids dive in and paddle out, with nary a towel-warmer in sight, I was reminded how suffocating city living can be for kids and their budding independence. As Monte swung onto his board and paddled out after them, I sat for the next two hours on the beach as if I was watching a slow game of tennis – I couldn't take my eyes off Monte as he attempted to ride those enormous waves. Out the back of the surf is one of the few places in the world where young and old, rich and poor, tall and small matter little. There's a sense of belonging that comes just with having paddled there. If you ever watch a surfer's funeral ceremony you will see it up close. I often think about funerals when I watch Monte surf — though I could probably say that about a lot of things I watch Monte do. I wonder if the paranoia will go away as he gets older. But with the hours I have spent sitting on a beach watching my small boy use his paddling-induced barrel chest to catch waves that could swallow him whole, I can't help but torture myself with what I would do and say if he wasn't ever to come back.

Nearly eight months later, after a winter's break from our Nipper lectures, Monte says he wants to join. As much as we would like to take the credit for his change of mind, it's not because of anything we have droned on about. It is down to positive peer group pressure. With footy season over, Nippers is next on the social calendar. After just a month of chilly October Sunday mornings watching fiercely competitive ten-year-olds with Bronte stamped on their lycra-clad bottoms trying to beat each other to the piece of hose stuck in the sand, and swim through serious swell further out than I have ever ventured, we agree to buy Monte his dream fibreglass surfboard for Christmas. But it is not just his Sunday morning life-saving lessons that push us towards this rite of passage, it's also the weekday board training sessions he is religiously attending. Run on a voluntary basis by one of the Nippers' dads a couple of afternoons and a few mornings a week it is a healthy and positive environment for the boys and an example of an old-fashioned community spirit that is threatening to fade away.

Our mornings always seem so burdened by breakfast and getting the knots out of Lucy's hair that we suggest Monte goes for the afternoons. But how to get him there? Both Roberto and I work fulltime — and my week-life is governed by a daily newspaper deadline that does not leave time for nipping out to drop my son at Bronte beach — but we decide to wing it anyway. Week by week we scramble to organise Monte's travel to board training. If I have worked Sunday, which happens every two weeks, then I try to organise my day off on a board training day. Sometimes Roberto can leave work early, but mostly it is through the kindness of

Monte's friends' parents.

In early December we are ready to buy Monte his fibreglass surfboard. Surfing with anything more than a body is not Roberto's department, so I call up an old surfer boyfriend who was Monte's and my neighbour during the three years we lived on our own. Monte vaguely remembers him and Grant hasn't seen Monte for six years but is happy to be part of Monte's boyhood transition. So we head down to Manly on Sydney's northern beaches to look for boards. I've no idea what Grant and the salty-haired 14-year-old shop assistant are talking about because I don't speak their language.

I turn to Mont and whisper, 'I am so glad Grant is here. I would have chosen your board based on its colour.'

'Yeah, I know,' he answers without taking his eyes off the two boys.

I went in with a budget of $250 and come out having spent $335. It would have been $370 but Monte went halves in the cover. It is a cool board, I am told, and a little bit bigger than planned, at 6 ft instead of 5 ft 8 in. It was custom-made as a sponsorship board for a 16-year-old called Kai Otton. We even get to see a picture of Otton riding Monte's board. And then we go surfing, of course.

It takes a couple of weeks for Monte to find his feet (or 'feeting' as he tells me it is called), one of which I spend apologising, day after day, for not having enough time to take him down to the beach. But during the second week of the board's new life Monte and I meet in the kitchen at 5.40 am each morning, chuck on our cossies, he grabs the board, I grab my sunnies, and we drive the few minutes down to Bondi Beach. The sun has just risen and there are only about four people with boards in the water. Everyone else is walking the length of beach. I've never been to the beach at this time before and it's a whole other world, full of people, yet truly peaceful. I just sit and watch Mont because I am not prepared to leave him for the walking brigade just yet. It brings back memories of when I was a teenager and would loyally sit watching my boyfriend surf the day away — until I discovered windsurfing, that is, which was the perfect complement to his surfing. If there was an onshore wind, the surf at Manly would be flat but the harbour would be great for windsurfing off Balmoral Beach, so he would come and watch me. If there was an offshore wind Manly would pick up, and I would go and watch him.

Monte finishes his surf with an awesome ride and as he gets out he shakes his hair, grabs his board and runs up the beach to me. Oh my god, I think as I watch this familiar ritual, I used to go out with you.

After three days of going down to the beach at this time I notice the strict routines that take place. The old guy in the red board shorts walks past me as he laps the beach at exactly the same time each morning and the young girl who jogs from 6.10 am to 7 am changes her swimming costume every day. We get noticed, too, having joined what seems to be a club. The tattooed veteran on a long board, or Malibu, comes out of the surf on day four and smiles at me saying, 'He's very keen, your little one'.

Then I change jobs. I leave the newspaper to fill in as editor for a year at a magazine, as the editor is taking maternity leave. It is a transfer, as both have the same parent company, but whether I will go back to the newspaper, stay, or go on to do something else, I haven't decided. I have been at the paper for four years and as I've said, it's not family friendly. It's not just the hours, it's the stress, too. The change means I can take Monte surfing after work — and without having to drink alcohol first.

One summer Friday evening the heat is unsupportable, so Monte, Lucy and I head down to the beach. The swell is big and it's crowded out the back. Lucy, who is dressed for a Channel crossing with her gingham bikini under her pink one-piece, purple goggles and yellow bubble tied securely around her bulging belly, waves her big brother goodbye as he zips up his steamer (a full-length wet suit) before turning to surf on Monte's old boogie board, safely on the sand.

I can't even sit down this time because the minute Monte paddles out I lose sight of him. Not just because the waves are so big — I mostly can't see anyone, but when I can see them there are so many I can't make out my son. Roberto is meeting us at the beach at 7 pm. It's now 6.30 pm and I can't wait any longer for Roberto, so I approach a man about to head into the surf.

'I am sorry to do this, I know you are going out there to surf, but my ten-year-old is out there and I can't see him. Could you keep an eye out for him? He's in a black steamer on an Aloha board.'

'He'll be fine,' he says. 'What's his name?'

'Monte.'

Five minutes later Monte surprises me. He's come out of the

surf about 50 m south of where I was desperately searching for him. 'What?' he asks.

'What do you mean, what?' I ask back.

'Some guy came up to me in the surf and said "Are you Monte? Your mum wants you." Don't do that to me, mum.'

And with that he went back into the water — heading, it seemed to me, for a different group of guys, guys who didn't know his mother sent out search parties for him.

surf's up

Surfing can be an expensive hobby but there are ways around it: you can buy a second-hand board and wetsuit and, while private lessons are expensive, one or two in the early years are a worthwhile investment.

parts of a surfboard

NOSE This is the front tip of the board, which is often pointed but may be rounded, especially in larger boards such as a Malibu. Because of the potential danger of a sharply-pointed nose, a plastic cone or nose-guard is often fitted.

TAIL This is the back end of the board and comes in a number of different shapes, all of which are designed to give certain performance characteristics to the board under specific conditions. Since the surfer's rear foot is placed close to the tail, and is a major factor in manoeuvring the board, different shaped tails affect the response of boards to different surfing techniques.

ROCKER This is the term given to the upwards curve of the board along its length. It plays an important part in the board's response to turns and other tight manoeuvres.

DECK The top of the surfboard, as with a boat, is called the deck and is the part you stand on. The deck of a new board is very slippery, so wax or grip must be used to prevent your feet slipping off when the board is wet.

RAILS This is the term given to the side of the board where it curves over from the deck to the bottom. Most surfers grab the rails to help them jump to their feet when the board takes off on top of a wave. Leaning or 'edging' the rails into a curve can assist with turning the board in tight manoeuvres.

FIN The fin is the protrusion under the tail of the board. It acts like a rudder, helping to stabilise and steer the board through the water. Modern surfboards may have one, two or three fins. Fins come in different shapes and sizes depending on the needs of the surfer or the design of the manufacturer. The difference lies mostly in the performance of the board: a single fin is best for good sweeping turns whereas twin fins are generally better for tight cut-backs or re-entries. Most short boards these days have two fins.

LEG-ROPE PLUG This is a small socket in the deck of the board close to the tail and contains a securing device into which the end of the leg rope is fitted.

buying your first surfboard

A 'coolite' or 'foamie' is the perfect board to start on if you are a grommet (young surfer). It is made of buoyant foam, covered with material to give your feet something to grip on to. They start from around $100. If you have been surfing on a foamie and feel confident enough to surf outside the flags, then you can upgrade to a fibreglass board.

It helps if you ask experienced surfers where you should go to buy a surfboard, as I did for Monte, because it is easy for people selling secondhand boards to hide damage and make the board look like new. The experts advise not to buy from newspaper ads or surf supermarkets.

So, go for a specialist board dealer who has a wide range of new and secondhand boards, and ask his or her advice. You can pick up second hand fibreglass boards from around $100 to $500.
The main thing to look for in a secondhand board are breaks or 'creases', which can indicate permanent structural damage. Make sure you examine all dings and blemishes carefully — minor ones can be repaired. Avoid buying boards with lots of dimples.

Bigger boards that are thicker and wider provide more stability, but your weight and height need to be considered (so remember to weigh and measure yourself before heading to the shop). A board with a fuller nose is easier to paddle and is better for a beginner — but it does make it harder to get through the waves than a board that has a fine, pointed nose.

other equipment

BOARD BAG AND NOSE GUARD You will also need a board bag to prevent your board from being damaged, and a nose guard to protect yourself and others from being speared by your board.

WETSUIT If you want to surf during the colder months you will need a wetsuit. It should fit snugly because it is the layer of water trapped between the suit and your body that keeps you warm. Water is a poor conductor of heat and therefore the water trapped against your body prevents your body heat from escaping.

Wetsuits can be difficult to get on because the arms and legs are very tight (designed to keep the cold water out) so use a plastic bag to help you get it on. Put the plastic bag over one foot at a time and pull the wetsuit on over it and it will slip on easily. Do the same with your arms. A full-length wetsuit that covers your arms and legs is called a steamer and is suitable for cold climates. If it is late summer when you get your first board you will need a spring suit, which has short arms and legs. A spring suit is a good investment (less expensive than steamers) and will get you through most of the year.

RASH VEST A rashie is an essential. It is an anti-rash t-shirt made out of lycra and worn under your wetsuit to stop it chafing the skin around your neck and under your arms. It is worn inside-out, with the seams on the outside, to give your skin maximum protection. It's made from material that is anti-UV so can also be worn on its own during summer to prevent sunburn.

61

WAX Every surfer needs a supply of wax, which comes in little blocks. You also need a wax comb to rough up the wax when it becomes smooth after use, to provide a better footing, or to scrape off old wax prior to rewaxing.

bodysurfing

The skills required to become a good bodysurfer come from just one thing: practice. Spilling waves are best for bodysurfing, but if you can catch a plunging wave you can avoid injury by somersaulting out before it breaks. (For a full description of the three types of waves see pg 65.)

1   **As the wave is almost upon you, push off the bottom or start swimming towards shore until you feel the wave begin to lift and carry you.**

2   **As the wave breaks, take a breath, put your head down and kick hard until your body breaks through. Your feet should be together, your back arched slightly and your arms extended in front of you. As the wave becomes steeper, tilt forward and surf along the wave's face.**

3   **You will probably have to paddle a bit to hold your position on the wave. Try to keep your body straight.**

4   **As you approach the beach, pull out of the wave by turning your body away from the wave's breaking force, or do a jackknife dive and let the wave pass over your body.**

Source: Surf Lifesaving Australia

surfing with a board

Expect to fall off a lot. That's all I can tell you first hand. Beyond that I have no experience of surfing, whatsoever. However, I have flicked through Monte's surfing magazines, listened in on his various surfing lessons and been the teenage girlfriend of a waxhead. This is what I gleaned.

You have to train so the moves become second nature. This will be a lot easier if there isn't any water getting in the way. Head for the beach and push the fins of the board into the sand to protect them from being snapped off (you might feel a little stupid surfing on the sand but it's a well-accepted rite of passage within the surfing community).

Lie face-down on your board with your hands placed at chest level and your feet hanging over the end of the board. Do a push up, keeping hold of the rails (sides of the board) and spring into position — one foot forward and the other at the board's tail (end) so you are in a crouching position with your arms held out to the side and facing sideways. One foot should land about halfway up the board and the other about a third of the way. Practise this over and over until you can make the move in one clean action.

The first time you do this, have a look at which foot automatically lands in front. If it is your right foot then you are goofy-footed. If it is your left, you are what is called 'natural'. It's the same as being right- and left-handed; whatever feels comfortable will work for you.

Once it's time to head out into the water, only go as far as chest-height because you are looking to catch a broken wave which will give you some control over your inaugural ride.

Hold on to your board, and with its nose facing out the back (not towards the shore) wait until the broken wave is at least 10 metres away. Point the nose to the shore, hop on and start paddling as hard as you can.

Let the wave pick you up and push you along. If it leaves you in its wake then you weren't paddling hard enough or may have been lying too far back on the board's tail. If you are picked up but nosedive, you are lying too far forward. If you're on the wave, just enjoy the moment and experience what it feels like to be taken along by the force of the wave. Do this until you feel ready to stand up.

Once you feel you are ready, remember what you practised on the beach and put it into action. Experiment with what happens if you put more weight on your front foot or your back foot. Leaning on your back foot tends to send the board flying out from under you, while leaning on your front foot will cause you to nosedive or else slow down. Now all you have to do is follow practise with practise. Have fun.

duck diving Once you feel confident enough to tackle unbroken waves you need to know how to get out the back. You can either ditch your board as you dive under the wave, assuming you have a leg rope attached, or you can duck dive. Duck diving is the most common method used by surfers to make their way through breaking waves and the technique you need to master is:

1   **As the oncoming wave moves down on you, quickly draw your knees up so that you are effectively in a kneeling position on the board.**

2   **Just before the wave strikes, push the nose down hard and at the same time lower your head and shoulders so you literally dive under the wave.**

3   **As the wave passes over you, push the board down with your knees so that your body passes under the breaking wave and pull the nose up.**

4   **If you have handled the manoeuvre correctly you should bob up behind the wave without having gone backwards too far. Start paddling again and repeat the manoeuvre with each wave until you are through the break.**

what forms a wave

Waves are caused by wind blowing over the surface of the ocean. The longer, stronger and further it blows, the bigger the waves will be. There are three kinds of waves:

PLUNGING WAVES OR DUMPERS Plunging waves break with tremendous force and can easily throw a swimmer to the bottom. They usually occur at low tide when the sand banks are shallow and there is less water for the waves to break onto. This wave type is dangerous and is a common cause of spinal injuries.

65

SPILLING WAVES Spilling waves occur when the crest or top of the wave tumbles down the face or front of the wave. As the tide gets lower and the sand bank on which the waves are breaking becomes shallower, this type of wave will form tunnels or tubes. Generally, spilling waves are the safest waves.

SURGING WAVES Surging waves may never actually break as they approach the water's edge, as the water is very deep beneath them. They do not lose speed or gain height. Surging waves can knock swimmers off their feet and carry them back into deep water. For this reason they can be very dangerous, especially around rocks.

rips

A rip is a strong current running out to sea. Rips are the cause of most rescues performed at beaches. A rip usually occurs when a channel forms between the shore and a sandbar, and large waves build up water that then returns to sea, causing a drag effect. The larger the surf, the stronger the rip. Rips are dangerous as they can carry a weak or tired swimmer out into deep water.

identifying a rip The following features in the surf will alert you to the presence of a rip:

✳ **darker colour, indicating deeper water**
✳ **murky brown water, caused by too much sand stirred up off the bottom**

* smoother surface with much smaller waves, alongside white water (broken waves)
* debris floating out to sea
* a rippled look, when the water around is generally calm.

To escape from a rip, Surf Lifesaving Australia advises:

* not to panic and stay calm.
* if you are a strong swimmer, swim at a 45 degree angle across the rip and in the same direction as the current until you reach the breaking wave zone, then return to shore.
* if you are a weak or tired swimmer, float with the current, don't fight it. Swim parallel to the shore for about 30 – 40 m until you reach the breaking wave zone, then swim back to shore or signal for help.
* remember to stay calm and conserve your energy.

surf safety

Make sure you are wearing the appropriate wetsuit to keep yourself warm – a rash vest for summer, a spring suit (short arms and legs) for cooler months and a steamer (full length) for winter.

It's important your leg rope is the right length. If it is too long you could get tangled. If it is too short your board will boomerang right back at you. Check with a reputable surf shop if you are unsure of the correct length.

If there aren't other people surfing, don't head out for a surf unless you've got someone watching you from the beach. Something as simple as a leg cramp can prevent you from making it back to shore alone. The other concern is that your board may hit you on the head.

Don't think you have to go for every wave. If one comes along that looks too big to handle, let go of your board and dive under – your board will follow if you are using a leg rope, if not you can always collect it from the shore.

Don't surf once the sun goes down because it is too hard to see clearly and no one will be able to see you. Also, there is a higher risk of sharks being on the prowl.

Being dumped is part of the deal and most probably won't cause you any harm if you go with the flow. The most important thing to remember is to stay calm. If you panic you will use all your energy trying to swim out of an engulfing dumper and in such a state you may not know which way is up. It's better to relax and wait for the wave to pass over you and then swim to the surface.

wave talk

WAVE HEIGHT height of the wave, measured in various ways
in different surfing zones

CREST top of the wave

TROUGH depression between two waves

FACE front of the wave

BACK rear or back slope of the wave

WALL steep, sheer face of a rearing wave

BARREL a tunnel or hollow under the crest of a wave as it rolls over

TUBE another name for a barrel

FAT WAVE a thick, sloping wave with no wall and often a broken crest

HOLLOW WAVE a wave about to break with a concave face

CLOSED OUT a wave that breaks evenly along its entire length

LEFT-HANDER a wave where the break is on the right of the surfer

RIGHT-HANDER a wave where the break is on the left of the surfer

POCKET point at which the break is at the top of the wave

ORDINARY poor surf

MESSY broken surf

CRANKING good surf

LIP top edge of the wave

SHOULDER unbroken part of the wave next to the break

SUCKING bottom of the wave drawing back

books to read

Mark Warren's Atlas of Australian Surfing *Mark Warren*
Handy for planning all those holidays that include the surfer in your family as well as being informative about the conditions you are likely to face once you get there. It also comes in a smaller traveller's size.

Surfing: the Fundamentals *Jeff Toghill*
Written by a surfer for surfers, Toghill's book was useful for both Monte and us. Monte read about techniques and enjoyed absorbing the culture of the sport while we learnt what to look for when buying his board.

The following are novels I bought for Monte when he stopped reading, hoping they might pique his interest as they focused on his beloved surfing. As I haven't read them, I have included the publisher's summary on the back cover though Monte tells me they are all 'alright'.

Riding the Waves *Theresa Tomlinson*
When Matt goes to visit old Florrie as part of a school history project he doesn't expect to enjoy himself. He would much rather be down on the beach with the young surfers he hero-worships, riding the waves — if only he had a board. There's a lot more to Florrie, though, than meets the eye.

The Wave Rider *Graeme Lay*

Surfing, its risk-taking and sheer exhilaration, is the backdrop
to this timeless story of love, betrayal and reconciliation. *The
Wave Rider* explores the tensions of two young people as they
seek to fulfil their conflicting ambitions.

Lockie Leonard *Tim Winton*

Lockie Leonard, hot surf-rat, is in love. The human torpedo has
barely settled into his new school and already he's got a girl on
his mind. And not just any girl: it has to be Vicki Streeton, the
smartest, prettiest, richest girl in the class.

Surfers *Matt Griggs*

Characters, innovators, adventurers, big wave maniacs, world
champions and freakish talents, Matt Griggs captures the true
spirit of today's surfers, profiling 26 of the world's most
interesting and inspiring souls.

Surf's Up *Diana Chase*

Matt and Brad, two outsiders, team up in this Margaret River
surfing classic. Grommets and legends, mateship and mishaps
— as awesome as riding your first wave.

pets

Monte and I had a routine when he was little: after reading him a story I would tell him something about when I was a little girl. Some stories were make-believe, some were true experiences and some were a combination of the two. This routine lasted for about a year and began because his father and I separated. Monte had just turned one and was naturally spooked by the change. The five or ten minutes I spent storytelling were meant to reassure him, and me, that life goes on. I found particular comfort in this because parenting can be so in-the-moment sometimes — it is best not to stop and think about the Herculean task you've taken on otherwise you might panic and freeze. Pilots, gymnasts and prime ministers must feel the same.

As he was heading off to sleep one night, I told him the true story of how he got his name. When I was a little girl I had a Golden Labrador whom I loved dearly. He would walk my sister and me to school, and be waiting at the gate when it was time for us to walk home again. He didn't do it because he had to, but because he wanted to. He didn't do anything he didn't want to. Like the time my dad threw him in a friend's pool because no one had ever seen him swim. Well, the reason no one had ever seen him swim was because he didn't like swimming. Instead of performing he just slowly sank to the bottom and calmly stood there on his four legs playing chicken with my dad. He won because my dad dived in, brought him to the surface and helped him out. He shook his short coat and lay down next to me in the sun to get warm again.

'I learnt a lot from Monte,' I told my Monte, 'and secretly promised myself I would name you after him.'

Just as I finished telling this story Monte, naturally, asked for a Labrador. And I, naturally, said no. But that didn't stop him from asking and asking and asking for a pet, any kind of pet, during the three years it took me to meet Roberto, and the ensuing six months before we married. Until then I hadn't relented for even a moment because contemplating any more responsibility just freaked me out. Being a single parent with a one- then two- and finally a three-year-old boy had its moments but I consciously kept our lives simple. Our relatively smooth lives threatened to become unmanageable if we had to live with some animal.

But with Roberto I felt that extra bit secure and slowly saw myself as a potential pet owner. Monte must have smelt this because his requests became more frequent and my arguments more hollow. Around his fifth birthday, after great discussions, Roberto and I gave in to the pestering, though not without compromise. And Monte really loved Occie, his huge dead octopus who had a bed in the fridge and a Tupperware pool for parties in the garden. But sadly Occie could only live with us for three days.

He stank. But we did the whole pet burial thing and then went back to the fish shop and got Prawnie.

With both Roberto and me working full-time, we tried more than ever to encourage Monte to give up his pet quest. 'You don't want to have happen to you what happened to Amelia, do you now?' I would ask rhetorically. 'I wouldn't let that happen,' he sang back. But it was an academic argument. I knew I couldn't give Monte a dog, and then take it back to wherever it came from a month later because I had been lumped with looking after it. I would just be lumped with it. So I blocked my ears as he pressed on, driven by a firm belief he had got the raw end of the deal in the pet department. He tried all avenues, such as talking about quirky websites he'd found, one of which included a quiz telling you what type of dog suited your lifestyle. Perhaps we wanted to have a go?

His hard work and determination finally paid off thanks to an advertisement in the school newsletter: a family of silkworms needed a new home. As I read it out to Monte you could see by the look on his face he thought it sounded glamorous and mysterious, as would any six-year-old boy. So we agreed to adopt them. Unaware of any advancement in the care and breeding of silkworms over the decades since I had kept them, we went with the traditional method. One shoebox filled with mulberry leaves covered with cling wrap with holes punched in it. They all turned grey and died within the week. Monte wasn't too upset because he was used to dead pets.

Still not satisfied, however, he got smart and changed tactics.

His ninth birthday was approaching, as was an opportunity to emotionally blackmail us into giving him a pet. We really wanted to say no because — why change now? But we thought it was time to give the guy a break. He had proved his commitment to the cause, asking regularly for eight years, putting up with dead pets, fast-dying pets and cleverly working out how to emotionally blackmail us. So for his ninth birthday Roberto and I broke with tradition, and a couple of live guinea pigs moved into Monte's room — which soon started to smell a lot like the Easter Show. But it wasn't until we moved house two years ago that we entered the big league. We got chickens. Again it was a compromise, because Monte would love to get around on a tractor but as we live in a high-density Sydney suburb he can't. So we got chickens.

Having no idea where to buy live chickens I started searching through the phone book and made a few calls. Like any potential owner of a purebred dog or cat, I wanted to know our chickens were coming from a good home. Guided by how nice the chicken owners sounded on the other end of the phone — which would naturally correlate to how happy their chickens were — I made my decision. I liked the man from SF Barter and Sons, located at Eastern Creek, west of Sydney. Roberto was busy with his cinema season so we went with Greg, our neighbour, as we planned to share the chickens and eggs. On perhaps the rainiest day in January, we set off for Eastern Creek to buy our chickens.

We slipped around in the mud looking at all the different chickens before deciding to choose one of each colour — red, white and black. We bought some grain and eggs that had been laid that day, and home we all went. We hadn't built the chicken's house, so the yet-to-be-named girls lived on our front porch — in what probably seemed like a detention centre — while their new home was being built out the back, again by Greg. But before they moved in we had to name them. Lucy, Monte and Greg got to choose a name each. Lucy chose Paula after Paul, her favourite daycare teacher, Monte chose Pamela because he was going through his *Baywatch* phase and Greg chose Shirley because neither Jo, his partner, nor I, would let him call the red chicken Jo or Sarah, so Shirley seemed appropriate.

Paula, Pamela and Shirley moved into their chook house along with Fly and Bear, the guinea pigs, who are both female despite their names. We had no idea if they would all get along, but going down the following day and seeing the pigs laid out on their fat little backs sunning their even fatter tummies, while the chickens busied themselves with scratching around in the dirt, you couldn't have dreamt up a more contented animal commune.

Wanting the new girls to feel at home, we thought it mean to keep them locked up, which was contrary to the advice Mr Barter had given us when we bought them for $16 each. He said to lock them up for at least a week, preferably two, so they become familiar with their home and learn that is where they go to eat and lay. When it came time to let them free range, we were advised to allow them only a couple of hours in the afternoon, just before sunset. We did this for three days, but they seemed so happy for the hour or so we let them wander around the garden, that the time stretched until they were free ranging all day. At sunset during the second week I went down to put them to bed, but couldn't find them anywhere. I looked in all the spots they had marked out as favourites but they had disappeared. About to panic, I happened to look up and saw them perched in the frangipani tree like a trio of overweight and excessively fluffy sparrows greatly enjoying a game of hide-and-seek. They looked thoroughly chuffed with their cleverness, and daintiness, as they sat on a bendy bough that threatened to snap under their enormous weight. So we went back to locking them up, which was the only way we were going to get some eggs out of them, too.

Whenever we let them out now for long periods they eat so much grass there isn't room for pellets, and consequently they don't lay, because grass alone doesn't provide the energy they need. Just like us, chickens need a balanced diet.

We are very lucky with our neighbours who are so patient each time the girls scratch around in their herb gardens or neatly mulched beds. Because our four gardens all roll into one another, separated only by trees and shrubs, the chickens march across everyone's lawn. One afternoon there was a barbeque next door that we were unaware of, so had left the chickens to roam while we were out. As the guests arrived so did a dog who got the surprise of his life when he saw what he had to play with. We arrived home just in time to see people zigzagging all over the lawn trying to catch either chickens or a dog. Without Monte I don't know if we would have saved the girls because he was the only one confident enough to crash-tackle the chooks. Apparently, he and his friends do it all the time, or so he told us later.

Apart from an infestation of red mites — common to chickens, especially broody ones — Paula, Shirley and Pamela are wonderful company and hours can be lost watching them strut around the garden in single file with their matching coloured feet and feathers, clucking to each other comically as they scratch the soil looking for pesky insects and weeds to snack on. We love them a lot for their freshly-laid, warm, weighty eggs, fresher by days or even weeks than anything found in a store. Allowed to eat more grass and plants than their commercial cousins, our chickens' yolks are so fluorescent orange they look fake — and are closely correlated to the number of pavlovas we now eat (it's a quick way of getting rid of a half dozen, so goes my excuse). But I love those fluffy old birds most for giving me a break from the emotionally draining task of pretending I know things. Together Monte and I have learnt how to care for the girls. He told me their combs would change colour when they were preparing to lay for the first time. I told him they need to eat pellets and fatty meat only for the first few weeks to build up the energy required for laying. Letting them graze on grass all day is akin to filling up with junkfood, leaving no room for essential nutrients. He wondered about the subtext.

Then sadness struck across the street. Fluffy the guinea pig lost his partner and came to live with Fly and Bear because it is cruel to keep a guinea pig by itself. They are social animals and will cry if they don't have company. So Fluffy, the widower, moved in and brought with him a serious hutch. We put it in the chickens' enclosure and it looked like an enormous mansion within a gated community. The guinea pigs now come and go as if they are in the wilds of South America, because Greg cleverly built the chicken cage around the lime and mandarin trees.

Fluffy immediately brightened up the guinea pig girls' day, while also getting them pregnant. The delivery of the first pups, a couple of months later, made for a classic David Attenborough moment. Monte watched them being born while relaying the details to me at work over the phone. It was a moment we had been waiting anxiously for because I had read up on pregnant guinea pigs and to my horror discovered they shouldn't have babies after they're 12 months old. Well, our girls were definitely older than that because we had had them for a year, and when we got them they were no spring chickens. Terrified we were going to kill them by allowing them to get pregnant, I took them to the vet. I explained I had read that pelvises of older guinea pigs can fuse together and prevent them from giving birth, and asked if he could feel around and tell whether Fly and Bear could deliver. The vet duly felt around but unfortunately couldn't tell if they had fused pelvises or not. My options, he told me, were to keep an eye on them and when they went into labour I should whip them up to the vet for an emergency caesarian if they looked like they weren't doing well. Otherwise I could book them in for an elective caesarian a week before their due date. I think he found it hard to keep a straight face while telling me all this, but he doesn't know Fly and Bear like we do.

I went home and talked it over with Roberto, basing my pro-caesarian argument on the premise that it came down to a value judgment: one family's guinea pig is another's dog. Guinea pig caesarians aren't cheap, at around $300 each, but we did consider it — or I did anyway. But in the end nature took its course. Thankfully the girls were still of childbearing age and successfully delivered four pups between them: Fly, one; Bear, three. But our happiness over the addition to the family was short-lived because they all disappeared. We weren't sure how as there was no evidence. But when it happened again, months later, we found out.

After the stress of wondering whether the girls would make it through labour we had Fluffy promptly de-sexed. But it seems he wasn't to be the problem. One of the baby pigs had already got both girls pregnant. This time they had two pups each and we kept a watchful eye on them, but at 3 o'clock one morning Roberto heard frantic barking. He thought the chickens were being attacked, so he went to investigate and chased two big black dogs out of the enclosure. He could see the chickens were OK and assumed the pigs had been too scared to come out of their hutch.

He went back down at first light to make sure and saw Fluffy and the babies lying stiff in different corners of the enclosure. Bear and Fly were safely tucked away in the corner of their hutch. We don't know if Fluffy was being brave and trying to protect the girls, or whether he was stupid enough to think he could take the dogs on. Whichever, we said our goodbyes around the burial site, next to the fish pond made from a bath tub. Roberto and I braced ourselves for the kids' reactions. Monte was sad, expressing himself with a shrug of one shoulder, while Lucy told anyone who would listen that our guinea pigs were dead. *Dead*, she would repeat, a little louder and with wide eyes, loving the drama of the word.

'On a brighter note,' I told Mont as we finished feeding the animals together a couple of days later, 'we don't have to worry about the girls getting pregnant again.' And then Fly went pear shaped. Followed closely by Bear.

We lost those babies, too, but this time we worked out why. Magpies love nicking black underwear (from the clothesline) and, so it seems, baby guinea pigs. They swoop down and pluck the little babies from the cage. Bear and Fly are safe because they are too big to be snatched. So that's that, we said to each other. No more babies. We are back to where we started. Except Fly started to grow and on Valentine's Day gave birth to two little girls. So now we have Fly, her gorgeous girls and Aunt Bear all happily living together in the late Fluffy's hutch. Greg has put a roof on the enclosure and Roberto has tacked shade cloth around the bottom so the little ones can't squeeze through — and we are all thankful to have retired from breeding guinea pigs.

After eight years of banging on about wanting a pet, you would think there would be no argument over Monte caring for the animals. But there is. He grumbles more often than not and wants to know why Lucy doesn't have to help. We come up with something reasonable as an answer but are ignored while Monte tricks, bribes or threatens Lucy into helping. I don't know why he bothers because they only argue all the way down to the hen house about who will change the water, measure out the grain and chuck around the food scraps from last night's dinner — chickens so love meat or seared tuna with a coriander marinade. But they are a steadfast team against Roberto's threats to ship the pigs back to South America and the chickens to the butcher. I'd like to see what he would do if the kids called his bluff.

keeping chickens

Paula is white, a cross between a White Leghorn and an Australorp. She, like most white hens, is bossy and dominates the hen house. Unlike the other breeds, Paula has never gone broody (she doesn't want to sit on her eggs and hatch chicks) because it's not in her nature. We always know when Paula has laid because her eggs are paler than the others — being a white chicken means she doesn't produce as much pigment.

Pamela is a Black Australorp and black chickens are prone to broodiness, particularly with the onset of warm spring weather — they need warmer temperatures to successfully hatch their chicks. When Pamela goes broody we place her in a cage with a wire bottom, and a small bowl of food and water, so she can't get comfortable. After a week, and once her body temperature cools down, she is meant to go back to laying. But sometimes this can take a couple of weeks if she isn't eating much while in the wire cage. Chickens need good, healthy food, with lots of calories for energy to lay eggs regularly. So, to get Pamela laying again we fatten her up with fatty bits of meat, mince or bone dust, pasta or oil that has had meat cooked in it. We add the oil to the laying pellets so she will eat more of them. The oil makes the pellets more appealing than the bland cardboard I'm sure they must taste like.

Shirley is the red hen, a Rhode Island Red. She only went broody after Pamela did, which made us suspect she was just copying to get out of having to hang around with bossy Paula on her own. But we didn't have to put her in a cage; we threw her off the nest each day and locked the hen house so she couldn't get back in. We did this for a couple of days only, so Paula wasn't prevented from eating, drinking and laying. We kept an eye on Shirley in case she made for the nest once we opened their house again, but she didn't.

Because we got the three girls together, they have grown up with each other and so tolerate one another, but mixing breeds can be fraught with difficulties due to their different natures. Rhode Island Reds and Black Australorps need more food than White Leghorn crossbreeds, but the white chickens are more aggressive and tend to get to the food first, so the red and black chickens miss out.

our chicken house We built the chickens' house from bits and pieces found in rubbish piles. An old door became the coop's floor and metal legs taken from an old desk raise it off the ground.

Other pieces of wood form the back and sides while the roof is corrugated iron insulated with a piece of wood to stop it getting too hot or cold. We placed smaller pieces of wood as the front walls, to make it dark, which chickens like, while leaving an opening for them to come and go. Then we painted the whole coop with waterproof exterior paint and put in a perch (an old didgeridoo) for them to sleep on. A long piece of wood juts out from the front and the girls jump onto it to get into their house. Alternatively, we could have built a ramp, but because the guinea pigs live in the same enclosure, we didn't want them wandering up the ramp into the chickens' domain. The house and run area is surrounded with chicken wire supported by posts and a gate.

We let our chickens out for a couple of hours most days to graze around on the lawn finding insects, grass and worms to feast on. When you first bring your chickens home, however, it is important to keep them locked up for a couple of weeks so they get used to their new house and fill up on pellets and calorific foods needed for laying. If you don't do this, and let them graze too early, they will fill up on grass that provides no energy for laying. It's their equivalent of junk food.

food Chickens need laying pellets as their staple diet but getting good quality pellets with lots of calories is difficult. Most brands have had all the goodness removed. Trusted brands include Vellas or YSF (Young Stockfeed). Don't bother with pellets found in a pet store as these will be the least nutritious. Instead, look for a rural produce store, and they do exist in the suburbs (our closest one is Kensington Produce at Botany). But even these pellets may not be the best quality. The most important ingredients in laying pellets are protein and calories. If they are not getting enough calories, chickens won't have the energy to produce an egg nor to lay it. There was a time, 15 to 20 years ago, when backyard poultry farmers didn't need laying pellets because meat and three veg dinners were cooked every night at home, so there was enough around to keep chickens living happily off kitchen scraps, and laying. But with smaller families, and fewer families, backyard poultry farmers have created a market for laying pellets. Our chickens love eating corn, cheese (especially ricotta), pasta (full of energy), tomatoes, bone dust from the butcher and rice.

Try to avoid pellets that are pale in colour, because they aren't good quality. Eating them would be like eating only bread and water every day. But if these are the only pellets available, then you can add some used oil that has had meat cooked in it to their bag (a 40 kg bag needs around 3 cups). Pour it over the top and let it soak through. Keep an old jar in the kitchen and every time you cook with oil, tip it into the jar to pour over the pellets. Adding pieces of cooked meat and meat fat to your chicken's food dish will add another energy source. By doing this you provide enough calories for them to lay regularly. An alternative is the organic laying mix that our chickens love, and makes for healthier eggs, but it is twice the cost of normal pellets. Bread is another favourite among chickens, but be careful about how much you give them because it contains a lot of salt. A couple of slices a week is plenty.

A sure sign your girls aren't getting enough food is if you find them waiting at the gate or fence of their house when they hear you coming. (But they will leave food they don't like, so don't mistake this as a sign they are not hungry.) Another sign they aren't getting the nutrients they need — other than not producing eggs — is an increased amount of chicken poo under their perch in the morning. This occurs because the chickens are eating a lot of extra food to try and get the nutrients they need. Their bodies then have to work overtime to get rid of it. Chickens need more food when temperatures drop. A pinch of chilli powder in their feed will help them if they have caught a cold.

red mites We've had our chickens for over a year now and the only disease we have had to battle is the common red mite. These are tiny pinhead-sized mites that are grey until they become engorged with the blood from the chicken, and then they turn red. Red mites feed on the birds at night and live in the perch, nest or crevices of the chicken house. The life cycle is speedy because they hatch in two days and reach maturity in five days. We kill them by regularly cleaning out the chicken coop and spraying the entire structure with diesel fuel, a natural product that won't harm the animals. We spray once every couple of months, or more regularly if the mites are still hanging around. This happens when the girls are stationary on the nest for long periods because they are broody, so the mites have a field day and their populations explode.

By using wood chips suitable for animals, rather than straw, you can keep red mite populations down as they love nesting in hollow straw, something they can't do in wood chips.

TIPS

* check with your local council as to how many chickens you are allowed to keep in your backyard. Some councils don't allow roosters.

* chickens love having dustbaths, which is when they roll around in the dirt, much like a dog, and fluff up their feathers to let the dirt cascade over them. Dustbaths are also important to prevent ticks and mites from breeding in their feathers. Make sure there is enough loose sandy soil in their run area for them to do this.

* hens will start laying from around 20 weeks and live for six to eight years.

* a pullet is a young laying chicken.

* if summer days are exceptionally hot, gently hose your chickens down to cool them off.

* chickens need to be wormed four to six times a year. You can buy chemical worming liquids that are mixed into their water but then you can't change the water until they drink it all, so only give them a small amount of water when you add worming liquid. Or else follow the Italian example. They add raw chopped garlic to mince or rice. One garlic clove per bird every three months should be sufficient.

keeping guinea pigs

The perfect first pet for small children, guinea pigs are soft and cuddly and become used to people quickly if they are cared for properly. They require daily maintenance to keep their water clean and food fresh. Their cage should be cleaned out once a week.

Guinea pigs are social animals and should never be kept alone. It is best to keep guinea pigs from the same family or else rear them together from a very young age. If you can't find another guinea pig to live with yours then you must find it another sort of companion. They can live happily with rabbits and chickens, but they will always love another guinea pig most.

Before a guinea pig can be taken away from its mother it should be fully weaned, so aged between six and 12 weeks. To make sure the guinea pig you are buying is healthy, there are a few checks you need to make:

* **a six-week-old guinea pig should weigh around 250 g (9 oz), be plump and look well-fed.**
* **its coat should be shiny, sleek and without bald spots.**
* **its skin should be smooth but not dry.**
* **the ears should be clean, eyes bright and teeth not overly long.**
* **hold the guinea pig close and listen to its breathing to make sure it is not wheezing.**
* **lastly, make sure you check what sex it is so you can decide whether you want to breed them, or not.**

Put a male and female together and you are guaranteed to have babies before you know it. To determine the sex, carefully pick up the guinea pig and hold its back legs and bottom in one hand with its tummy facing up. Gently press down above its genitals. If it's a boy a penis will pop out and if it's a girl it will have a Y-shaped opening.

our guinea pig house Guinea pigs need lots of space and some commercial cages are just too small. It is easy to build them a cage of their own so they will be happy. Place an old wooden box with a small opening inside a large frame covered with chicken wire, but make sure the wire's holes are small enough so the guinea pigs can't squeeze out — you may be surprised at what a fat guinea pig can slip through. They will use the box for sleeping and hiding, and the open area for running around. The enclosure should have a door that can be bolted safely shut so other animals can't get to them. You can move the cage around the garden, if you have lawn, so the guinea pigs always have fresh grass (they make great lawn-mowers). If you decide to do this, and don't build a floor for their running-around section, ensure the cage is secured into the lawn so it can't be tipped over by another animal or children. If you don't have a garden guinea pigs will happily live on a balcony, in a garage, or even in someone's bedroom. The cage can have either a wooden or plastic floor covered in newspaper and a thick layer of wood chips (suitable for animals) that help soak up the urine.

their food Hay, lucerne and fresh grass complemented with a seed mixture suitable for rabbits and guinea pigs are the most important items in a guinea pig's diet, along with fresh water, of course. They also love lettuce, cucumbers, tomatoes, watermelon, apples and oranges, the latter providing them with a good source of vitamin C. They hate potatoes and onions. If you offer a bowl of grain each day, plus a handful of hay or lucerne for each guinea pig and a varied supply of fresh food from the list above, your guinea pigs will love you. Remember to remove any pieces of fresh food that haven't been finished, as they will go mouldy and will make your guinea pigs sick as well as attract ants and other insects.

Water is best offered in a water bottle that is attached to the side of the cage and delivers drips of water when nudged with the guinea pig's mouth. Regular cleaning of the water bottle is important to prevent a build up of algae that will make the animals sick.

their babies It is possible for a female guinea pig to have five litters in one year, so it is best not to breed them unless you intend to go into the guinea pig business.

If you do find yourself with a pregnant guinea pig, you can expect her babies to arrive in around 68 days. Between one and four babies will be born in each litter and arrive fully developed with eyes open, hairy and ready to eat solids, though they do suckle for two to three weeks. But be warned, guinea pigs reach sexual maturity very early: females at five weeks and males at seven to eight weeks, and a mother guinea pig can become pregnant again as early as 12 hours after delivering her pups.

A mother and her babies should be left alone for at least five weeks. If you watch them you will see how affectionate they are as they rub noses together and snuggle up close.

their sounds Insistent squeaking translates unmistakably to begging for food, while faint or timid peeping and squeaking are the sounds of a fearful and lonely baby. Guinea pigs kept on their own will use this peeping sound to express their need for human contact. When you stroke and cuddle a guinea pig it will make a cooing sound that means it is feeling calm and relaxed.

silkworms

There are four stages to the life of a silkworm: egg, larva, pupa and adult. Eggs hatch in about six to 20 days and the larva, the silkworm caterpillar, will eat for about 26 days before spinning silk. It takes about three days for it to fully spin a cocoon and turn into a pupa. The moth, or adult stage, emerges from the cocoon after around 21 days. Two days later the moth lays its eggs.

There is only one food a silkworm will eat — mulberry leaves, and they must be fresh. Make sure when you pick leaves that you don't pull off whole branches because the leaves will grow back more quickly if you leave the branches intact. If you keep your freshly-picked leaves in an airtight bag or container in the fridge they should stay fresh for around five days. You don't need to bother with water because silkworms don't drink. They get their moisture from leaves, which is why they must be fresh. By keeping the silkworms' home tightly covered with cling wrap, with a few air holes, the mulberry leaves will stay fresher for longer.

I have never seen silkworms spin silk. But apparently they do. If like mine, yours never perform, the following checklist might help:

* **make sure their house is clean and not littered with dead leaves or droppings. Clean it every couple of days otherwise mould will form and this kills silkworms.**
* **don't try and keep too many. If they are squashed together they can't feed properly. The rule of thumb is to keep 30 within the space of a 30 cm (12 inches) diameter circle.**
* **don't disturb them if they do start spinning because they won't make a cocoon. Instead they will punish you by turning brown, then black, and dying.**

When first laid, all silkworm eggs are lemon yellow. After three days they turn white, if they are infertile, or black, if they are fertile. Fertile eggs might hatch in around two weeks after being laid in the middle of summer, but they usually won't hatch unless subjected to 'winter' in your fridge for at least several weeks. Wait until the eggs turn black before putting them in an airtight container in the fridge. Once you take them out of the fridge they will hatch in six to 20 days, or maybe not at all. Direct sunlight in the morning for a few hours will hasten the hatching.

books to read

My Family and other Animals *Gerald Durrell*
> Durrell is a joy to read as he tells the story of his childhood
> spent studying animals and living on the island of Corfu in the
> 1930s. This book could well be responsible for creating more
> than a few naturalists.

Backyard Poultry: Naturally *Alanna Moore*
> This is not a readily available book via bookstores but is easily
> bought over the internet (visit a search engine, such as Google,
> and type in the book's title and author). Moore is well respected
> and offers answers to questions such as what to do if a broody
> chicken won't get off her nest to feed, and how to treat red
> mites with a natural product. Well worth owning, along with a
> couple of chickens.

The Official RSPCA Pet Guide: Care for Your Guinea Pig

Guinea Pigs: A Complete Pet Owner's Manual *Barron's*
> These are the two books we used for learning how to care for
> Bear and Fly and their pups. They differ at times because
> Barron's is published in the UK and the RSPCA's book is
> Australian but both are handy resources and answered all
> our questions.

gardening

The childhood memories that intrigue me most are like bread and milk — they're always available, no trouble to live with, and, on the surface, appear harmless. I find them intriguing because I wonder how true they are. Are they so easy to remember because they've become fiction? And if so, why the adaptation? Did something cause the script to change? And if so, why is that not part of the memory?

A nursery story that, curiously, pops into my head with little prompting falls into this category. I remember it well, though don't own a copy of it — and this makes me suspect that I may have rewritten it.

An old man and his wife lived happily together. They always wanted children but hadn't been blessed with them. The old man went to work every day while his wife stayed home. One day the old man discovered to his delight that his wife was pregnant. They jumped for joy, hugged and kissed each other. The pregnancy progressed perfectly except for one thing. The wife had a terrible craving for strawberries, not just any strawberries, but those from the mean man's garden next door.

'But sweetheart,' the old man said, 'he won't give us any strawberries.'

'I have to have those strawberries. You have to work out how you can get them for me,' replied his wife.

So the old man sat by himself at their wooden kitchen table later that night while his wife slept. Staring out the window, which framed the sleeping strawberry patch, he decided to take a risk, steal into the night and collect strawberries for his wife.

When she woke the next morning her husband presented her with the stolen strawberries in the hope their taste would end her craving. But it had the opposite effect. She became more and more demanding now she knew her husband could get her those delicious strawberries. So each night he would wait until she — and, hopefully, the mean man next door — were asleep before climbing the stone wall and picking a bucketful to take home. Everything was going well until one morning his wife woke to find herself alone in her house. The mean man next door had killed her husband after catching him stealing his strawberries.

This is the first thing I thought of when Monte arrived home with a bunch of parsley, tomatoes and carrots after playing in the back lane of our old house one school afternoon. He told me an old man, Alfred, gave them to him, and said Monte was welcome to more whenever he wanted. After a couple of weeks of random offerings from Alfred I started to wonder if Monte was stealing the fruit and vegetables, so asked him to show me where he was getting his supplies from.

So we walked through our garden, to the back lane, and along two houses to Alfred's. A tall wooden fence, full of splinters and faded by years of seasons, hid the meandering pathways and tangle of plants that fed Alfred, and, now, occasionally us. I was both embarrassed and fascinated by this discovery. Alfred had lived in our street for some 40 years, after arriving in Australia from Italy, and told me he had always grown basketfuls of fresh fruit and vegetables. But this was the first I knew of it, despite six years in the same street. Alfred didn't garden from a book; he didn't need to. He had brought to Australia his childhood experiences of growing up in Italy with a back garden that had, instead of a neat lawn, plants that fed people. And all the knowledge he needed for his small Australian plot grew with each passing year. A particular passion was his tomatoes — he believed decades of work meant his were the best you would ever find.

'You could grow them, too, if you wanted,' he generously offered. 'All you need is one of mine, slice it thickly, lay it on a couple of pieces of newspaper and leave it in the sun for a month or two, making sure it doesn't get rained upon. Once the slices are totally dried, carefully store them, still on the newspaper, until it's tomato planting time, and then just lay the newspaper, along with the dried tomato slices, on top of your well-fertilised soil, cover with a thick layer of rich compost and wait. Then thin the plants once they push their way to the surface.'

It took us two years and a house move three blocks south to get around to it. But by then, sadly, Alfred had gone. I often thought about Alfred's garden, and Monte's friendship with him, and wished I too could potter around growing food and teaching my children all I discovered. But there never seemed enough time — until last summer. With Roberto ensconced in his outdoor cinema, the kids and I had four weeks of holidays to ourselves. We may have had time, being on holidays, but it wasn't the right time for starting a vegetable garden, which we discovered while shopping for seeds. Arriving at the local nursery smack bang in the middle of a season meant our choice was limited to a variety of cucumbers, carrots and lettuce (we didn't need tomatoes as we were finally going to plant the variety we called 'Alfred' after buying one from an organic grocer). But we weren't going to be stopped by something as insignificant as a lack of variety. What held us up was history.

I was kidding myself if I thought Roberto was going to dig up the lush lawn we'd pegged out for our two-single-beds-sized garden before March. After a week and a bit of waiting, it became clear I was going to have to ask for help elsewhere. So our generous neighbour, Greg, spent an early, hot, Sunday morning digging up the grass. I certainly appreciated his help, but should have taken more notice of when he chose to do it. Monte and I nearly melted under the midday sun as we sat sifting through the soil, weeding out rocks and roots. I also wish now I had heard of Esther Deans.

Wanting to garden from scratch I bought packets of seeds instead of seedlings. Big mistake. Sure, it was quick work when Mont, Lucy and I sprinkled the carrot seeds into the little troughs we had scooped out. But once they poked through, it took many more hours to pull out clumps of carrot tops carefully, separate each fragile seedling, and replant the needle-thin stalks with enough room for each to grow. Not that they went on to grow, because root vegetables don't like being transplanted. The cucumbers were a much easier task because their seeds were bigger and, following the instructions, we only had to plant four in each hole. Sowing the lettuces probably fell somewhere in the middle — although I am not exactly sure of this, because I didn't see it happen, but Monte says Lucy opened the packet and walked around the patch with it.

It certainly looked like a vegetable patch, thanks mainly to the signs Monte made from balsa wood that sat proudly ahead of each bare row of soil. And so what if Roberto thought they were burial crosses? If the rain hadn't washed away Monte's beautiful water-based paintings Roberto surely would have picked them as species identifiers.

From a summer's holiday project, gardening has grown to become a perennial activity in our family. We are now two seasons into vegetable gardening and love it. It didn't matter that the summer plantings weren't a patch on our winter crop — actually, *failed* would be more accurate — because our vegetable patch has become more than just a source of fresh vegetables. It's why the amount of garbage we put out each week has shrunk (thanks to food scraps going into the compost) and it's a magnet for end-of-the-day people weary from kindergarten, school and work.

Sometimes we take it in turns to go down, other times we find ourselves down there together, but wandering around its messy borders, admiring its progress, can make up for a day full of defeats.

Mind you, we didn't feel this satisfied after the inaugural planting of our summer crop. Ignorant of the first rule of gardening — run a garden north to south for maximum sun — we got a lot of cucumbers but nothing else grew higher than freshly-mown grass. Unfortunately, without Roberto around, Monte and I were able to jump in feet first. Lucy looks like she'll be joining our feet-first team. Roberto can spend weeks reading instruction manuals, but then will find us engrossed in something entirely different because we got bored waiting. Put us all together and you have a working team. But without Roberto, we didn't take the time to discover that carrot seeds should be mixed with fine sand, in a sealed glass jar, with small holes punched in the lid so they can be sprinkled evenly along the soil. And we didn't stake the cucumbers early enough so they could train themselves up the poles — poles that were too thick, anyway, so the cucumbers' tiny tentacles couldn't possibly reach out and slither their way to the top. We also staked the cucumbers at the front of the patch, leaving the carrots (by design) and lettuce (by accident) behind with little chance of basking in the sun. Probably the only thing we did right was pick the male cucumber flowers, and rub them against the female flowers ensuring a bumper crop of headband-shaped cucumbers (they need room for dangling to grow straight and, yes, sex came up).

But once we pulled up our dwarf crop, and mixed in the rich compost we had created, we were left with soft, dark organic soil and lots of lessons learnt. But I still hadn't heard of Esther Deans. So I went ahead, with the children and Roberto, turning the soil, digging in extra animal manure and picking out weeds before planting our winter crop. With timing on our side this time, we could choose what we wanted, so in went carrots, beetroot, celery, broccoli and cauliflower. And this time we chose seedlings, instead of seeds. It's quicker, results are more guaranteed and the kids loved running around the nursery picking out their plants. Roberto built a small, practical fence around the plot so the chickens wouldn't march through eating juicy young shoots.

Everyone loves an excuse to get dirty, so finding eager helpers each weekend to pull out weeds, wave around water and chuck in fertiliser was never hard. I would spend half an hour each evening with a drink in one hand, hose in the other and one or two people by my side telling me what they had done that day. Ten weeks passed and we started to prepare for harvesting. We were so proud. The broccoli and cauliflower had finished growing all the necessary leaves for cocooning the green and white vegetable heads to come. And budding specimens could already be seen when the heart of the leaves was gently revealed. Spidery green fountains spouted from each carrot top and a couple had orange mounds pushing through, a sure sign they were ready for picking. The celery was a lush, green dense mass of leaves and stalks, encouraged by regular picking. The only obvious casualty were the beetroot — they never grew any bigger than a golf ball. Don't know why.

For ten weeks our garden had been growing, just as the books said it should, and for ten weeks the chickens happily snapped off the grass that grew between the posts of Roberto's fence as they strolled about the garden. But in the eleventh week, as if planned, all three girls neatly jumped the fence and ate every single leaf from every single broccoli and cauliflower plant, leaving long, thick, bare, scarred stalks with Borrower-sized vegetables perilously perched on top. Our only consolation was knowing that the week's eggs would be extraordinarily high in iron. Dying to pick something, and looking forward to the intense taste a freshly-pulled carrot promises, we dug up a few. And we weren't disappointed: they tasted sweet, fresh and minty-orange. But, boy, were they stumpy, really stumpy. So stumpy they were as round as a passionfruit and about as long. It took a bit of digging to find the answer to that one: the number of rocks and stones in the soil was stopping the carrots' roots from neatly drilling downwards. That left celery as our sole achievement, though out of soup season there is only so much celery you can consume, so the guinea pigs got lots.

It might not sound like we have had much success, but I am not sure that is the point with gardening. It's simple fun and if something works in the garden it seems like a bonus, or maybe that is just a novice's perspective. Whichever, when I look back on our first two seasons I remember them with as much satisfaction as I now get from the garden — now I know about Esther Deans and her easy instructions for a very successful no-dig garden.

During the 1970s, Esther wrote a wonderful book called *Growing Without Digging* and it has been reprinted many times over. I happened to find a copy in a secondhand bookstore. It shows how, with bales of straw, lucerne, compost and animal manure, you can make your own garden on top of grass, concrete, wood — anything. Which means anybody can do it anywhere and you have a guarantee of goodness for your plants without having to wonder if your soil is high in nitrogen or low in potassium or other tricky (and for me, almost unidentifiable) elements. This method is also ideal for growing carrots and potatoes.

If you are building a no-dig garden on top of lawn or an old vegetable garden, use wet newspaper as your base. But if you are building on top of concrete or a rocky ground, first put down an 8 cm (3 inches) high layer of old leaves, small sticks and even seaweed, then add the newspaper. You'll find a full description of how to build Esther's no-dig garden at the end of the chapter.

Along with our neighbours Greg and Jo, following Esther's instructions, we built a shared no-dig garden during winter that was bountiful. We ate 24 delicious lettuces that were replaced with seedlings each time a row had been eaten, so there was always another lot on the way. And this time the beetroots took root, (again, I don't really know why) and were delicious when wrapped in foil, drizzled with a little olive oil, sprinkled with sea salt, and roasted in the oven. We planted corn seedlings (we didn't offer them enough sun so they died — the whole garden needs at least six hours a day), but the herbs — basil, coriander and parsley — randomly dotted in between, were as successful as the forest-green spinach, which made many delicious Sunday night spinach and filo pies.

Ironically, after such a success, we haven't planted another garden. It's because of this book: writing now takes up most weekends, so I just can't fit it in. But I really miss messing around in the garden and one of the things I am looking forward to once this is finished is planting a vegetable patch again. I read widely on gardening while experimenting with ours, but keeping a journal about your own garden is the best tool for learning what will and won't work. And Lucy absorbed more about gardening than anyone realised. With her grandparents, she visited their neighbour who has a serious vegetable garden on their acreage. She asked to have a look, being a gardener herself, and happily wandered around, trying to identify all the plants (some of which she knew), casually eating their beans as she went.

Monte, meanwhile, has big plans for our small space. He talks of growing one type of vegetable at a time so he can sell vegetables on the footpath, and we don't doubt him. A couple of years ago he made a small fortune selling avocados from the tree in Ann's garden (Alfred's next-door neighbour). And Monte is not sentimental: even Ann had to pay. He also knows the power of a cute Lucy, after taking her door-to-door with endless boxes of fund-raising chocolates. 'Sure, you can do that,' we say. But first he has to grow the garden. And at that, he just smiles and says, 'Whenever you're ready, guys.'

107

before you begin

Gardening is a lot easier when you've got the right tools. A basic set is inexpensive and if cared for properly will last through many seasons.

* gloves with cotton backs and either leather or rubber palms (they are much cooler and allow more flexibility than all-leather gloves)
* spade, for a large garden
* small trowel for planting seedlings
* hose or watering can, depending on the size of your garden. If you need a hose then you will also need clip-on spray attachments
* gardening clogs or boots if you are going to tramp around in the dirt
* secateurs for pruning and harvesting
* hoe for turning the soil and preparing garden beds
* lightweight mattock for digging up the soil
* rake for sweeping up leaves to use as mulch
* compost bin if you want to make your own fertiliser for the garden.

preparing your vegetable bed

Draw a diagram of your garden, including your house or other nearby buildings, and record where the sun falls during the day.

You don't want a garden drenched in shade, as you need at least six hours of full sun every day to ensure your vegetable garden thrives. Once you have decided where your garden will grow, draw it to scale and measure how much space you will have available for planting. For example, if you want to grow carrots, lettuce, beetroot, spinach and cauliflower, you need to find out how much room each vegetable will need, then calculate what will fit in the space you have allocated before you begin.

Ensure your garden runs north to south for maximum sun exposure and, if possible, with an east- or north-facing wall to provide a climbing area for peas or beans, and extra warmth after it absorbs the sun's rays during the day.

The first thing you need to do is work out what kind of soil you have. The lighter the colour of the soil the sandier it probably is, the darker the better. Sandy soil doesn't hold water, or powdery fertilisers, so add lots of 'humus' (moisture-retaining organic materials). Humus includes grass clippings, animal manure, compost, leaves and wood shavings (which are expensive unless you recycle them, as we do, after the chickens and guinea pigs have finished with them).

If your soil resembles clay, it will hold too much moisture. To counter this, mix lots of grass clippings into the top 20 cm (8 inches) layer of clay, with about 1 cup of lime powder for every metre.

Once you have prepared your garden bed, leave it for a couple of weeks — if you have the time — to allow weeds to pop up so you can pull them out. This saves on weeding time later.

building a no-dig garden

A no-dig garden built on top of grass, concrete or rocky ground means you don't have to dig up lawns, pull out weeds, care whether your soil is heavy with clay or dry and sandy, or sift it for stones. To build a no-dig vegetable garden, first designed by Australian gardening enthusiast, Est-her Deans, in the 1970s, you will need the following ingredients:

* **newspaper, and lots of it, but definitely not coloured paper or cardboard**
* **a bale of lucerne**
* **a bale of straw**
* **animal manure (preferably poultry)**
* **compost (if unavailable, use topsoil)**

A no-dig garden is made up of rectangular or square patches, rather than rows, so build whatever shape you want for each variety you plan to plant, using bricks, railway sleepers or pieces of hardwood.

Each bed will be layered with the materials above but as I've mentioned, your base will determine what you start with. Damp newspaper can sit straight on top of grass, but concrete or rocky ground needs a layer of old leaves, sticks and seaweed (available free from the beach or else bought from a nursery), built 7 – 10 cm (3 – 4 inches) high.

Over the base (either grass or leaves, sticks and seaweed) you layer lots of wet newspaper pages. Overlap the wet newspaper so there are no holes, until it is at least 1 cm (¼ inch) thick. This prevents grass and weeds pushing their way through.

Next spread out a thick layer of lucerne, water thoroughly. Then sprinkle manure, water thoroughly and add at least 20 cm (8 inches) of straw. Water thoroughly, before laying more manure. Esther says to top this off with a thick layer of compost, about 7 – 10 cm (3 – 4 inches), to plant the seeds in. If you don't have any compost you can buy topsoil from a nursery and mix through the required amount of blood and bone for the plot size you are working with.

Again, thoroughly water your no-dig garden. Then it will be ready for planting as if it was a freshly dug garden bed. It is worth making compost (or topsoil) mounds for each seed planting to ensure all the necessary nutrients are close by. Mounds can be individual for large seeds, such as cucumbers, or patted into rows for smaller seeds, such as carrots and lettuce.

After a season, and harvest, your no-dig garden will have melted into a rich bed of composted soil. To plant another crop, you only need to thoroughly water it before adding another layer of compost, or manure.

If you plan to grow a climbing vegetable — such as beans, peas or cucumbers — hammer the supporting stakes into the grass after you have laid out the newspaper and before you spread the lucerne. If your no-dig garden has been built on concrete or rocky ground you may want to buy a teepee-shaped trellis, or else balance three stakes together and secure at the top with heavy duty string.

Potatoes are a perfect crop for a no-dig garden because they can be laid within its layers. When it comes time to harvest, you just lift the straw and pick what you need. Ensure potatoes are always covered with straw, otherwise they will turn green and poisonous.

fertilisers

There are three main elements in fertilisers:

* nitrogen (N) for healthy leaf growth,
* phosphorous (P) for root development, flowering and the formation of fruit and seeds, and
* potassium (K) which helps develop strong stems while playing an important part in healthy growth. Sandy soil is likely to be deficient in potassium.

Because we have chickens, we've a ready supply of chicken manure, which is considered one of the best animal manures as it has the highest content of NPK nutrients. But it can never be used 'fresh' on the garden because it is too rich. We regularly collect the chicken manure and either chuck it in the compost or leave it in a bucket for three to four weeks until it has had a chance to break down.

If you prefer a powder or granular fertiliser, choose granular over powder because it is less likely to blow away. Never add more than the directions state and always mix into damp soil. Check the information on the fertiliser pack for its specific ratio of the three elements. Leafy vegetables, in particular, need a fertiliser with lots of nitrogen.

composting

Composting is easier than you might imagine, but it is not as easy as simply burying your scraps in the garden and waiting for them to break down (because both carbon and nitrogen are necessary for the process to work). You can throw almost anything into your compost except meat, which takes too long to break down and rots. Eggshells and human hair are two excellent ingredients for rich compost. Materials high in carbon include newspaper, wheat straw, sawdust and chipped wood products. Nitrogen is found in animal manure, urine, grass clippings and green prunings from plants. Lucerne straw and grass clippings contain both carbon and nitrogen. The *Yates Garden Guide* suggests a ratio of 1:1:3 for leaves, sawdust and animal manure, using a wheelbarrow as a measurement guide.

Other necessary ingredients for producing valuable compost are sun, moisture and air. If you have made your compost correctly, it will generate its own heat, rather than relying on the sun. But check it doesn't become too dry and, if necessary, add enough water to keep it moist (if it's too wet it will be too cold to work its magic).

You can use a store-bought compost bin, a large plastic bin with the bottom cut out or use fine chicken wire to make a tall cylinder — and fill it with food scraps on a daily basis. Keep the compost bin covered with either hessian sacks, sticks and leaves, or a lid with air holes. Dampen every 30 cm (12 inches) of kitchen waste material with a hose, then add animal manure or a sprinkling of lime to prevent flies and weevils from populating your compost.

Seaweed is also an excellent source of minerals for your compost as are grass clippings and just-cut bracken that is still green (and so high in potassium). Avoid adding soil because it can suffocate the composting process.

how to make compost tea Use cheesecloth or muslin to make a compost tea bag about the size of a pillowcase. Fill a clean wheelie bin with water and drop your compost-filled tea bag into the bin and leave for two weeks. Remove the tea bag and use the compost tea as a liquid fertiliser to water your garden.

growing seedlings

Rather than planting seeds directly in the garden bed, you can raise seedlings to be transferred once they are big enough to look after themselves. This also saves time on thinning. Most books recommend using a seed-raising mix because it has the right balance of nutrients — and soil taken from the garden can often raise more weeds than seeds.

To grow seedlings you will need punnets, such as strawberry or margarine containers (make sure there are small drainage holes in the bottom). Fill each punnet with seed-raising mixture to just below the rim. Place in a baking dish of water (or another big, deep container that can be filled with water) and leave them until they have soaked up as much water as possible. Thinly sprinkle the seeds on top and cover with another light layer of soil. Bigger seeds can be pushed into the soil, though always follow the instructions on the packet about how deep and far apart the seeds should be.

You can either leave the punnets in the baking dish, making sure the water sits at the drainage level, or else provide daily, careful watering (remember, if the water spray is too harsh, fine seeds can get washed away). Seeds grown this way don't need full sun, and certainly won't withstand rain. They are ready to transplant when there are at least two pairs of leaves visible, though there is nothing wrong with waiting until they look like miniature versions of what is to come.

If you would prefer to sow your seeds directly into the garden, and you haven't built a no-dig garden, make sure there aren't too many rocks or weeds in the furrows that will prevent the roots from finding their way to the damp goodness below. The soil must be damp, very deep down, so the day before you plant put the sprinkler on your patch if the weather has been dry. Mix small seeds, such as carrots or lettuces, with fine sand, and the seeds will automatically be spaced. A clever trick for creating furrows to plant seeds is to push the soil aside with the back of a rake, sprinkle in your seeds, then push the soil gently into place.

Seed packets come with instructions indicating how deeply you need to sow your seeds. If, however, you're using seeds you have harvested or dried (so there isn't a packet) the general rule of thumb is to plant a seed to a depth of 2 – 3 times its size. Too deep and the seed won't have the energy to force its way to the surface; too shallow and it could get blown away or eaten.

planting your vegetables

There are massive gardening books galore on every bookstore's shelves, so it would be impossible for me to give you all the gardening information you need in this one chapter. However, I can share with you what we learnt about a few of the vegetables we planted.

carrots These, like tomatoes, are well worth persevering with because once you taste a home-grown carrot you will find it hard to eat anything else. Even their colour is spectacular — deep orange to red. As mentioned earlier, the most important requirement for growing carrots is a soft, stone- and weed-free soil so the roots can travel downwards.

In the warm tropical zones of northern Australia carrots can be sown any time of year, but in the temperate zones, July through to March is best. For cold climates, plant carrots from August to February.

When mixing in fertilisers or organic matter to improve a clay soil, ensure they are well mixed in otherwise your carrots will grow forked and misshapen.

Carrot seeds need to be sown roughly 6 mm ($\frac{1}{5}$ inch) deep and should be mixed with sand to ensure an even spread along the furrows, which should be spaced about 20 – 30 cm (8 – 12 inches) apart. Seedlings take a couple of weeks to push through. They need a damp bed for this to happen, so mulch well with grass clippings to prevent your garden from drying out too quickly.

Once the seedlings reach 5 cm (2 inches) high, thin them out to 5 – 7 cm (2 – 3 inches) apart and throw away the excess seedlings. Do this again once they reach 15 cm (6 inches) high, though this time you don't need to throw any away because the roots should be big enough to eat, albeit skinny. Feeding carrots every few weeks with a liquid fertiliser (such as compost tea) will ensure faster growth. Avoid overfeeding, especially with a fertiliser high in nitrogen because you'll get lots of bushy tops and little carrot.

It will be three to four months before your carrots are ready for harvesting. For a family of four you need a row at least 4 metres long. If you want a continuous crop of carrots, sow new seedlings at four-to-six week intervals.

lettuces You can plant lettuces in your garden — or save the room for something else because a crisp, sweet lettuce grows well in a polystyrene box filled with a good quality potting mix. Sow a box once a month and you will always have lettuces available for eating. Move the box around the garden to make best use of the sun and keep it elevated if there is a danger of slugs, or chickens.

Lettuce is a summer crop that needs to be grown quickly in well-prepared soil that will hold, but also drain, moisture. It needs constant and thorough watering, every day in summer, and loves nitrogen (easily supplied by adding a mulch of grass clippings).

If you plant seeds, they should appear within a week, though be careful not to plant them when the weather is really hot, around 30°C (86°F), because they will have trouble germinating. A way around this is to dampen the seeds before laying them on absorbent paper towels and placing them in the fridge for a couple of days. Then plant as usual.

For a family of four, you would be wise to make 10 sowings every three to four weeks for a constant supply. Don't be scared to pick small lettuces, as these will be the crispest and sweetest, while making way for more planting. You can also pick a couple of leaves at a time for sandwiches.

cucumbers With their large seeds, cucumbers are easy to plant. In tropical/subtropical Australia, sow any time from July to March. In temperate areas the best months for sowing are September to January, while cold climates have only a short season, October to December.

Place four of the white seeds in a small hole and cover with warm soil; the warmth helps with germination. Each grouping needs to be at least 90 cm (3 feet) apart and will need a stake for the tiny tendrils to cling to, giving the plant support and height so the cucumbers can grow long and straight. They need a lot of watering to ensure you don't end up with bitter cucumbers.

If you don't have a big bee population in your garden you will need to artificially pollinate the female cucumber flowers. To do this, break off a male flower, which will have a stamen in its centre, and strip back its petals, then gently press it face-to-face with the female flower so the female pollen is transferred from the male flower to the female stigma. If you pull off the growing tip of cucumber plants you encourage side shoots and extra flowers.

Eight to twelve weeks later your cucumbers will be ready for picking. Four to five plants will feed a family of four.

potatoes Having tasted potatoes from Robertson, a small country town in the southern highlands of NSW, famous for its delicious brown carbohydrates, I was motivated to grow our own. I thought it would be as easy as waiting for one of my Robertson gems to grow a few eyes and then planting it in the garden. But it just rotted, as did my second attempt. So to begin with, it is probably worth buying a 'tuber' from a nursery — a disease-free potato weighing around 50 g (1½ oz) and with two or three eyes. And if it's successful, keep one aside to generate the next crop.

The easiest way to plant potatoes is to lay them on top of soil that has been loosened with a fork and thoroughly mixed with manure or compost. Cover with hay, straw or dead leaves to a height of 30 cm (12 inches) and top with manure or compost. Water well. If you want new (small) potatoes, pick them when the flowers appear by lifting the hay and taking what you need. But leave the plant, as it will keep producing potatoes that will be bigger for later in the season.

If you prefer to grow your potatoes in a garden bed, ensure lime hasn't been recently added because potatoes hate lime. Plant to about spade depth, 10 cm (4 inches) in well-drained fertile soil about 30 cm (12 inches) apart in rows 60 – 80 cm (24 – 31 inches) apart.

Lay a complete fertiliser mixture along the furrows using 80 g (2.8 oz) per metre (1.09 yards) (40 g (1.4 oz) on either side of the ridge). Place the tubers along the top of the ridge, fill in the trench with soil, ensuring the potatoes are covered, and firmly pat down.

Water generously and regularly and be ready to harvest in around 15 to 20 weeks.

how to make natural pest sprays

GARLIC SPRAY Deters aphids, thrips, cabbage white butterfly, caterpillars, snails, wireworms and some fungal diseases such as bean rust. Soak 85 g (3 oz) of chopped garlic bulbs in two teaspoons of kerosene for 48 hours. Add 600 ml (1 pint) of water and 7 g (¼ oz) of pure soap (not detergent). Strain mixture through gauze and store in a plastic container. To spray, dilute one part to 100 parts water.

MILK SPRAY Deters red spider mites, caterpillars and tomato worms. Dilute milk or sour milk with nine parts water.

SOAPY WATER Controls aphids, thrips, mealybugs, red spider mites and whitefly. Mix 30 g (1 oz) grated soap bar or two tablespoons laundry soap flakes (not detergent) in one litre of water. Leave standing until dissolved then strain through gauze.

an Australian sowing calendar

What you decide to plant in your garden will depend on the season and where you live. Australia has all the climate types: cold, temperate, subtropical and tropical.

	PLANTING SEASON	GROWING TIME
BEAN	mid-spring to late summer	10 – 12 weeks
BEETROOT	spring and summer	9 – 12 weeks
BROAD BEAN	autumn to winter	18 – 20 weeks
BROCCOLI	autumn and spring	10 – 16 weeks
CABBAGE	autumn to early winter	8 – 16 weeks
CARROT	early spring to early summer and early autumn	10 – 15 weeks
CELERY	spring and early summer	20 – 24 weeks
CAULIFLOWER	mid to late summer	14 – 16 weeks
CUCUMBER	mid-spring to mid-summer	8 – 12 weeks
LETTUCE	all year	8 – 12 weeks
PEAS(CLIMBING)	autumn and early spring	14 – 16 weeks
POTATO	autumn and early spring	16 – 20 weeks
PUMPKIN	mid-spring to early summer	14 – 16 weeks
SPINACH	all year (except mid-winter and mid-summer)	8 to 10 weeks
SWEET CORN	late spring to early summer	12 to 16 weeks
TOMATO	mid-spring to mid-summer	12 to 20 weeks
ZUCCHINI	mid-spring to mid-summer	8 to 14 weeks

This calendar is by no means a comprehensive guide to what grows best in each climate but it can be used as a starting point. To be certain about what you should be planting in each season, check with your local nursery or your state's department of agriculture for a planting calendar particular to your region.

good gardening

supply For a continuous supply of home-grown vegetables make small successive plantings and always leave a small section of the garden available for the next sowing.

herbs Plant herbs in your vegetable garden as their fragrance will keep pests away. Basil and parsley grow well with tomatoes while rosemary, chives and sage help keep carrots free from carrot fly. Chamomile, mint and dill encourage cabbages to grow. Petunias protect beans from whitefly, and comfrey added to your compost will speed up the composting process.

journal Keep a garden journal. After a few seasons you will find it better than any book for answers to problems in your garden. A lot can happen in a year and as much is forgotten.

warm walls If you can, plant your garden next to a wall. The sun will heat it up, adding extra warmth for your seedlings, and climbing plants can use it for support.

protect small trees Cut the bottom and top off milk cartons and put over small tree seedlings to protect them from birds and bad weather.

leafy vegetables With leafy vegetables such as celery, lettuce and spinach, pick leaves as you go and your plant will keep on growing.

tomato seeds If a friend is growing big beautiful tomatoes, or you see a luscious organic one in a store, you can use it to grow your own like Alfred. Cut the tomato into slices, lay on newspaper and allow to dry out completely. This may take a few months. Once the ground warms up in the spring, place your piece of newspaper with the dried tomato pieces into a foam box and cover with soil. Wait for seedlings to appear. Once they are big enough to transplant, thin them out then plant in soil rich with compost and prepared animal manure.

variety When planning your garden plant as many varieties as possible to safeguard against uncertain weather, as different varieties thrive under different circumstances.

bean and pea seeds When growing beans and peas, leave the biggest and best pod on the plant until it is fully mature and dry. Mark it with a brightly-coloured peg so when the plant has died you will be able to find your dried seed pod. Keep it safe for next year and you will have your own seeds.

123

books to read

Growing Without Digging *Esther Deans, 1990, Angus & Robertson, Australia (first published in 1977)*

> Probably a revolutionary idea when first published, Esther Deans shows, simply, how anyone, anywhere, can build a garden bed with or without soil.

The ABC Book of Gardening for Kids *ABC Books, 2001, Australia*

> Not so much a how-to, as an activity book with a focus on gardening.

Seasonal Tasks for the Practical Australian Gardener *Peter Cundall, Penguin, 1989, Australia*

> Peter Cundall is the well-known garden gnome who presents ABC TV's 'Gardening Australia' program. This book is very much a how-to for each month of the year, full of practical information and easy to follow.

Yates Garden Guide *Angus & Robertson, Australia*

> This is promoted as 'Australia's best-selling gardening guide' and is worth a place on any gardener's bookshelf. I enjoyed it for the insider's tips and hints that often answered the questions that regularly popped into my head as I was learning how to garden.

cooking

Peanut buttered crumpets with hundreds and thousands on top — that was what I ate in the bath when I was little. My children prefer frozen peas and a lime and soda. They like to defrost the peas in the bath as they eat them.

Kids are food freaks, whether it is because of what they eat or how they eat it, but they all love a meal served with predictability. Wednesday is pizza night in our house for everyone. It started because the American reality television show, 'Survivor', was originally on Wednesday, and, I was told, pizza and 'Survivor' went well together. I would like to be able to add that Sunday is both pancake morning and roast dinner night, and Friday is home to bubble and squeak, made up with leftovers from all the fabulous dinners I have thrown together during the week, but it wouldn't be true. The only tradition we have in our house is that we don't have traditions, just phases. Sometimes I cook every night, gathering hard to find ingredients and preparing lots of interesting dishes, other weeks it's just spag bol or chops. Now that 'Survivor' has finished we still have pizza night but it can be Wednesday, Tuesday or weeks between deliveries.

I don't remember many traditions in our house when I was

growing up, although one does stand out. Every second Friday
night for over ten years we would eat out at the same local
Chinese restaurant in Sydney's Neutral Bay. It was only every
second week because that is when we would be at our Dad's house,
my sister and I. The place is still there today, some 25 years later,
with exactly the same exterior — jade green tiles and big gold
letters spelling out its name, Mido Restaurant.

The Fridays we were due to go to Dad's dragged on forever
because all I could think about was that evening's delicious ritual.
My towering father would lead the way into the restaurant,
bellowing hellos to all the terrified waiters and waitresses who,
after nearly ten years of alternate Fridays, still couldn't bring
themselves to meet my father's twinkly, wrinkly blue eyes. But the
owner would always appear from behind the kitchen partition to
shake hands, squeeze our cheeks and welcome us, not that we
could understand anything he said.

Sometimes friends would come with us, but mostly we were on
our own and this we preferred. Not because we had our Dad all to
ourselves but because there would be more leftovers for breakfast
the next day. It took me years to give up the taste for last night's
honey prawns, spring rolls and sweet-and-sour pork for breakfast.
It has also been years since I have had Chinese — old-fashioned
beef-in-black-bean-sauce Chinese — partly due to the whole
healthy eating thing but mainly because my kids don't like
Chinese. Crazy kids.

So while we don't practise a Mido-style tradition in our house,

predictability is still dished up on a daily basis — I learnt long ago
not to bother to make the kids eat anything except what they like.
It's a waste of both food and time, because once they get a taste for
something my kids will want it every night, or day, though it
doesn't stop me from suggesting they try what we're having. Monte
has eaten so many chicken drumsticks in the eleven years he has
been alive I am surprised he hasn't grown breasts from the
hormones in the chicken. It's the same with his lunch. For the six
years that he has travelled down the road to the local public school
he has taken with him a vegemite sandwich, packet of chips and
an apple. To be fair, there were a couple of weeks when he had Sao
biscuits with butter and vegemite, because some other kid's lunch
had prompted him to ask for them, but otherwise it's been a really
boring bag — and that's just fine with him, and me too. It makes
for a quick morning, except when I go through one of my perfect-
mother phases. A recent one involved making the kind of lunches
a 'real' mother would make which include sandwiches with
numerous fillings and freshly baked somethings. I even bought
Monte a lunchbox, which was 'lame', I was told, but I already knew
that before I drove to the supermarket.

Kids don't want variety when what they thrive on is routine.
When I was at school, I had baked bean sandwiches, which just
went soggy, or vegemite and lettuce, or peanut butter and celery
sandwiches, and I hated the lot. I never understood, back then,
why you would tamper with a perfectly acceptable vegemite
sandwich on white bread. Sometimes I still hanker for fresh sliced

white bread spread with cold butter and tart vegemite. But all my childhood experience still doesn't stop me falling victim to the domestic goddesses who say, unless your kids have a gourmet menu that changes daily, depending on what fresh ingredients have arrived at the produce markets that morning, then you have failed them. The myth is perpetuated by magazines that annually run stories on cool ideas for your kids' lunchbox. It's not as if recess and lunchtime are designed for anything but playing, if you ask those who matter. All kids really want is something they like, that is quick to devour and fills them up. Seriously, who has plugged Lebanese bread with grated carrot and cheese, tuna and mayonnaise, lovingly wrapped it and popped it in the neatly labelled lunch box and not expected it to boomerang right back? Minus the lunchbox, of course.

Dinner time is no different. I could serve the same meal day after day and the kids would greet it with such gusto each time that you'd think they had waited all their life for two chicken drumsticks with paper towels wrapped around the ends, cold quartered tomato, four slices of cucumber (skin on), carrot for Monte and avocado for Lucy. I know I could do this because I do. Except when Lucy deviates and decides she is only having olives before bath time, frozen peas during bath time, and plain pasta afterwards. Or Monte sits in front of the television and eats so much raw spaghetti directly from the packet he becomes too full for breast-inducing chicken.

But to be truthful, I am the kettle who is calling her little pots black, because during Roberto's outdoor cinema season each summer I live on cornflakes — I have never been good at cooking for one. In fact, I am hopeless at cooking for two, too. And I seem to be on autopilot for four. So after spending 35 nights each year without a partner for dinner, it takes me a couple of weeks to get used to having someone at the table who doesn't get excited by cornflakes.

Sometimes I wonder — if we lived in one of those old rambling farmhouses with a kitchen the size of an inner city apartment, warmed by the glow of an open fire, would we sit as a family for more meals than we do with our uneven wooden table, surrounded by a bunch of mismatched chairs, at the centre of our small universe? I can imagine discussions of great importance taking place at our farmhouse table — things such as what Lucy is planing for Max, the three-year-old boy at her daycare who threatens to chop her head off. She wants to know if Monte will come to kindy and scare him off. 'Any time, Luce,' Monte says. (He does, in fact, happen to be with me one afternoon a couple of weeks later when I pick up Lucy, and she urges him to corner Max. But Monte need only look at Max and he is sorted.) But that's not what usually happens at dinner time. More often we are perched on sofas eating off laps, or squatting at the kids' wooden table and chairs. We still hear about Max, of course, and Lucy's plans for bringing him down, but her stories compete with television, newspapers, and washing, drying and folding — we very rarely 'put away'.

The universal complaint I hear is that food and kids don't go together. Real food, that is. But that shouldn't stop you from getting your kids to cook as cooking may instil in them a hunger for culinary culture later. From the time they can stand on their little wooden chair in the kitchen, with pint-sized utensils in their fat fists, small fry will love nothing more than making their own edible finger paints (see recipe at the end of the chapter). Thankfully modern day kids' recipes go beyond ham and pineapple pizza and chocolate sundaes. Donna Hay's *Cool Kids Cook* has a great stir-fry recipe that combines pineapple juice with honey and soy. But you don't have to use kids' styled recipes in order to get them involved. Just getting them into the kitchen is fun — and who knows, they may even like what they cook and want to eat it.

Working full-time with two children brings its fair share of guilt — and, before you say it, no amount of logic, reasoning or self-justification can change that. But I have found ways to reduce some of that guilt. So if there is something we can do as a family that everyone enjoys (although this probably means Roberto and me) it's more likely to find a home at our place. Discovering things the kids enjoy doing isn't the problem — the task is ensuring Roberto and I don't peter out midstream through boredom. Cooking together is one of those things that we all enjoy doing together. But be warned: once you introduce your kids to your domain there is no turning them back.

We've got Lucy on rotation, between our kitchen and our neighbour's, so you won't be surprised to learn I subscribe to the 'it takes a village' theory (Hillary Clinton wrote a book about bringing up children in which she suggested it took a 'village'). Last week

Lucy was next door lending a hand to hammer steaks. I don't know what was on the menu, but they sure got flat steaks. When she finished, she came home to annihilate cucumbers for our salad. (Nearly four, she has a special knife — but if you missed her in action and only saw the food she'd chopped, you could be forgiven for thinking it was a grater.) Then she helped put the chicken pieces, haloumi cheese and oregano leaves onto wooden skewers that then went to Monte, who painted each one with a mixture of lemon juice and olive oil before carefully barbecuing them. Neither ate any of it, but I didn't really expect them to. That is not the point of the exercise. If you think of cooking with kids as building their confidence rather than muscles, you may find your indigestion clears up. Or you can follow my father's advice (he's the only parent in the world I have ever come across who subscribes to this theory, but I like it) — whereas most parents urge their children to finish their meals — based on the logic that there are starving children in the world and it would be a waste to leave the food — my Dad thought the opposite. He would say to us that the food we didn't want would do more good in the garden than in our stomachs.

So, continuing my father's logic why not start a compost bin and, while you are at it, a vegetable garden? You don't even need a garden, pots do just as well (or check out the gardening chapter which shows you how to make a no-dig garden using concrete as your base). Kids love watching their vegetables growing, and will happily eat tomatoes and peas straight off the vine. It's only when vegetables come from a fridge that they seem to turn their noses up at them.

When I was in my early twenties, a young pregnant bride first time around, Samantha Stevens from 'Bewitched' must have been my idea of a perfect wife, judging by my behaviour. I tried awfully hard to be a 1950s housewife. It was scary. My then husband, who worked in advertising, just like Samantha's in the 1970s American sitcom, regularly invited clients home for dinner. Forget trying to be witty and charming — I was in way over my head! Alone, I cooked bad meal after bad meal. So bad our visitors couldn't pretend otherwise, not even for the sake of politeness. So I gave up cooking, disillusioned by the belief it was a genetically-acquired talent I'd missed out on. But then I grew up, left my husband, hung out with Monte for three years, fell in love, remarried and added Lucy to the lineup. I also started cooking again. Tentatively at first but growing bolder with each passing year. Now I don't mistake a failure in the kitchen for a personality disorder that renders me worthless.

I have seen an abridged version of my affliction in the short amount of time my kids have been hanging out in the kitchen. Monte needs lots of encouragement to keep at things he thinks he is failing in, and cooking both highlights this and offers a solution. With a little patience from me, along with his natural ability to problem-solve — if he has the peace of mind to use it — we can work through it. Together we have perfected the pavlova, after many aborted attempts. He loves the moment you turn the bowl, full of mixed eggwhites and sugar, upside down. If it doesn't slide out, you will have pavlova. If it does, you have a mess. Ours has yet to slide out, though we have had slippage, which calls for more beating.

Lucy and Roberto are the cupcake kings. Theirs are the fluffiest baby cakes you'll ever taste. No bias involved. Truly. I don't need to tell you that food is more than just a filler for empty bellies, but you may not know how its preparation is intrinsically linked to your emotions and sense of well-being. It is a lore of the kitchen that you can't bake successfully unless you're focused and free of emotional distress — which is, I think, why Roberto has cupcakes cornered and I don't.

You might even find opportunities to sneak in a little parenting when the kids are not looking. For example, following a recipe helps children to appreciate reading instructions (I wish), or you can introduce maths into the fun they are having in the kitchen — although I hope your attempts are more successful than mine.

'Hey, Mont, you know how you were doing fractions for homework the other day? Well, see this measuring cup, it's got fractions on it too.'

'Can I lick the bowl?'

'Hey, Luce, we have to make 12 biscuits, can you count how many we have cut out so far?'

'Can I lick the bowl?'

If you don't like cooking, or think you can't cook, there are always cooking classes designed for those who still have their milk teeth. Some are exotic, such as The Savour Chocolate and Patisserie School in Brunswick, Melbourne, that runs special cooking classes just for kids. There they learn to make gingerbread men (and women), strawberry tarts and chocolate éclairs. Even Otto, Sydney's glamorous Italian eatery, sporadically runs cooking classes for kids featuring fettucine with pomodoro sauce, otherwise known as pasta with tomato sauce. Whether or not you're creating a future Nigella or Jamie, the satisfaction that beams across a proud chubby, grubby face is what it's all about.

recipes

edible finger paints Stir 4 tablespoons of sugar and ½ cup of cornflour together. Add 3 cups cold water and heat over medium heat until mixture thickens. It will thicken further when it cools. Divide into four containers and add food colouring.

bath paints Mix 1 cup of clear liquid soap with 2 teaspoons of cornstarch. Divide into containers and mix in two drops of food colouring. Wash off walls and bath once the kids have finished.

cooked playdough Mix 2 cups of plain flour, 4 tablespoons of cream of tartar, 2 tablespoons of cooking oil, 1 cup salt and 2 cups of water in a saucepan and stir over medium heat for 3 – 5 minutes until the mixture congeals. Separate into three plastic containers and add food colouring as desired to each container. Allow to cool then knead the playdough until the food colouring is evenly mixed through and the playdough is smooth.

chicken and haloumi skewers

donna hay magazine issue 6, 2002

48 oregano leaves

250 g (9 oz) haloumi cheese, drained and
cut into twenty-four 2 cm (¾ inch) cubes

2 chicken breast fillets (400 g/14 oz) cut
into twenty-four 2cm (¾ inch) cubes

1 tablespoon olive oil

1 tablespoon lemon juice

sea salt and cracked black pepper

lemon or lime wedge to serve

24 bamboo skewers

Thread an oregano leaf onto a skewer, followed by a piece of haloumi, another oregano leaf and a piece of chicken. Repeat combination on each skewer with the remaining oregano, haloumi and chicken. Mix the oil, lemon juice, salt and pepper, and brush over the skewers. Heat a non-stick frying pan over medium-high heat. Cook the skewers, turning, for two minutes or until the chicken is cooked through. Serve hot or warm with lime or lemon wedges. Makes 24.

chop chop suey

Cool Kids Cook by Donna Hay

2 slices rump steak

1 tablespoon oil

1 onion, chopped

1 capsicum (pepper), chopped

1 carrot, peeled and chopped

2 sticks celery, chopped

200 g (7 oz) fresh hokkien or egg noodles

1 tablespoon cornflour (cornstarch)

¾ cup (6 fl oz) pineapple juice

3 tablespoons soy sauce

Cut fat off the steak and then slice the steak. Heat the oil in a large frypan or wok over medium-high heat. Add the onion and stir-fry for 2 minutes until soft. Add the steak and stir-fry for 2 minutes, or until brown.

Add the capsicum, carrot, celery and noodles to the frypan and stir-fry for 2 minutes.

Put the cornflour and pineapple juice in a bowl and mix well so there are no lumps. Add the honey and soy, then pour it all into the frypan. Stir-fry for 3 minutes or until the sauce thickens. Serve in bowls.

tacos

250 g (5½ oz) cheddar cheese, grated

¼ head of lettuce, washed

1 small bunch of coriander

½ cup sour cream

3 ripe tomatoes, diced

2 limes (if not in season use one lemon)

2 avocados

sea salt and cracked black pepper

1 brown onion

1 tablespoon olive oil

500 g (1 lb 1 oz) minced beef

1 teaspoon dried oregano

¼ teaspoon ground cumin

12 corn tortillas

Grate the cheddar cheese using the large holes on the grater and set aside in a bowl. A box grater is sturdy and easy for children to grip with one hand while they are grating with the other. A large chunk of cheese is best because it stops little fingers from getting too close to the sharp holes.

Lettuce is normally shredded with a knife for tacos but kids can tear it apart. Set aside in a bowl.

Pick the leaves from the coriander (warm fingers will help to release the oils in the herb) then carefully chop before setting aside in a bowl.

Place the sour cream in a bowl and set aside.

Dice the tomatoes and set aside in a bowl.

Remove seeds and skin from the avocados and mash with a fork then add the juice from the limes (this will keep the avocado from going brown). Add a little coriander and salt and pepper to taste.

Peel the onion and dice. Heat a heavy-based frying pan over a medium-low heat. Add oil and onion (the onion will sizzle if the temperature is right). Cook the onion for about 10 minutes or until it becomes translucent. If it starts going brown, reduce the heat and stir more often.

Add the beef mince and stir to combine.

In a small bowl, combine oregano, cumin, salt and pepper, then sprinkle over the beef mixture. Stir occasionally and cook for four minutes. When the meat turns brown it is cooked through, so transfer to a bowl and cover with foil to keep warm.

Heat oven to 180°C (350°F). Balance the tortilla shells upside down so as they heat they don't close. Place in the oven for five minutes.

Put out all the separate bowls on the table as if you were serving a buffet. Have fun putting together your own tacos. Makes 12 tacos.

pavlova

This is my own recipe, an amalgamation of various pavlova recipes I have unearthed.

The trick to making a successful pavlova is to use a scrupulously clean metal mixing bowl, metal whisk and beaters. If there is any grease or moisture on your equipment the egg whites won't stiffen properly. Using metal utensils helps because a chemical reaction between the metal and egg white strengthens the bubbles to produce a creamier and more stable foam. By adding vinegar and cornflour (a basic meringue does not include these ingredients) you get the well-known crunchy-on-the-outside, soft-on-the-inside pavlova. Also, once it has finished cooking, leave the pavlova in the oven until the oven has completely cooled. This will ensure a crisp bottom. Cooling it too fast can make the bottom go soggy.

6 large eggwhites

pinch of salt

300 g (9½ oz) caster sugar

1½ teaspoons cornflour

1½ teaspoons white vinegar

300 ml (10 fl oz) pouring cream

2 passionfruit to mix into the cream (optional)

Preheat oven to 150°C (300°F). Trace around a 24 cm dinner plate or cake tin onto baking paper and place the baking paper onto a baking tray.

Combine eggwhites and salt in the bowl of an electric mixer and whisk until stiff peaks form. Gradually add sugar, 2 tablespoons at a time, beating constantly, but gently, until the mixture is glossy and can be held upside down without the mixture falling out. If you overbeat the foam will dry out. Whisk in cornflour and vinegar.

Shape mixture on baking tray, keeping within the circle. Using a palette knife, smooth the mixture into a cake shape and remember to flatten the top.

Place in oven on the bottom shelf and immediately turn the heat down to 130°C (250°F) and bake for 1¼ hours (or until the outside is crisp but the inside is soft and chewy). Check by sticking a skewer in.

Turn off the oven and allow the pavlova to cool inside the oven until the oven is cold. This can take a few hours. Remove the pavlova and carefully peel the baking paper from its base.

Whip the cream. If you are using passionfruit, scoop the juice and seeds into the cream and gently fold together. Spread onto the pavlova and decorate with your choice of seasonal fruit such as a punnet of strawberries (halved, with the green tips removed) and three kiwi fruit, or a mixture of berries such as strawberries, blueberries and raspberries (one punnet each). Bananas are another option but they go brown after a few hours so only decorate just before eating.

The pavlova shell can be made a day ahead and stored in an airtight container. Depending on the fruit you use, leftover pavlova can be stored in the fridge for up to two days.

little cakes

100 g (3½ oz) self raising flour

80 g (2½ oz) butter

100 g (3½ oz) caster (superfine) sugar

2 eggs

Set the oven to 180°C (350°F). Place paper cases on a baking tray.

Sieve flour into a mixing bowl. Add soft butter and sugar, then eggs. Beat with a wooden spoon until soft and creamy. Add cherries (if you are using them), then put two teaspoonsful of mixture in each case (use less for smaller cases).

Bake 20 – 25 minutes for large cases or 10 – 15 minutes for smaller ones. Allow to cool on a cake rack and dust with icing sugar.

banana bread

1 cup sugar

¾ cup butter

2 eggs

2 cups plain flour

1 teaspoon baking soda

¼ teaspoon salt

1 cup mashed banana

½ cup crushed walnuts (optional)

⅓ cup buttermilk

Preheat the oven to 180°C (350°F). Cream sugar with butter. Add eggs and beat until very well mixed. Sift flour with baking soda and salt. Mix into creamed butter sugar and egg.

Add buttermilk and mashed bananas. If you are using walnuts, fold in crushed walnuts.

Pour into a greased and floured loaf tin lined with baking paper. Sprinkle with sugar.

Bake for 1 hour or until a skewer comes out clean when inserted.

basic stirred custard

donna hay magazine, issue 3, 2002

2 cups pouring cream

6 egg yolks

⅓ cup caster (superfine) sugar

1 teaspoon vanilla extract

1 tablespoon cornflour

Heat the cream in a saucepan over medium heat until hot but not boiling. Remove from the heat.

Place the egg yolks, sugar, vanilla and cornflour in a bowl and whisk until combined. Slowly pour in the hot cream, whisking continuously.

Pour the mixture back into the saucepan and stir over a low heat for 6 – 8 minutes or until the custard is thick. Serve warm or cold. Makes 2⅓ cups.

basic baked custard and rice pudding

donna hay magazine, issue 3, 2002

1 cup milk

1 cup cream

2 eggs

2 egg yolks, extra

$\frac{1}{2}$ cup caster (superfine) sugar

1$\frac{1}{2}$ teaspoons vanilla extract

freshly grated nutmeg

Preheat the oven to 160°C (325°F). Heat the milk and cream in a saucepan over medium heat. Combine the eggs, extra yolks, sugar and vanilla, and stir through the milk. Strain and pour into a 4-cup capacity greased ovenproof dish and sprinkle with nutmeg. Place in a baking tray and add enough hot water to come halfway up the side of the dish. Bake for one hour or until the custard is set. Serve warm or cold. Serves 4.

To turn your basic baked custard into rice custard, spread $\frac{1}{2}$ cup cooked rice over the base of the ovenproof dish before pouring in the basic custard mixture.

in the kitchen

preparation Nothing makes for success like being prepared. Read the whole recipe before you start to make sure you have all the ingredients and tools. Set out the ingredients on your work surface so they are within reach when you need them. Have them weighed out and prepared before you start.

oven Preheat the oven before you start cooking. It generally takes 15 minutes for an oven to reach the required temperature. However, oven temperatures can vary considerably so it may be worthwhile investing in an oven thermometer. They aren't expensive and could save you from wondering why your efforts aren't being rewarded.

You can leave an oven door open for at least a minute before the temperature drops, so don't rush when checking on your cooking as this is when accidents occur. If you leave the door open for longer than a minute, don't worry too much because an oven will return to the required temperature quickly after you close it. You can check your oven thermometer to make sure.

equipment Buy child-sized utensils such as whisks and spatulas so children can comfortably hold them in their hands. They will have more fun cooking if they can manage the equipment.

145

knives and cutting If children are confident enough to use a knife, remember a sharp knife is a safe knife because it won't slip off the food onto fingers. Have them practise cutting soft foods first, such as the inside of watermelon, zucchini or mozzarella.

If children are going to cut round vegetables, first cut them in half so they will sit flat on the chopping board and not roll away. If your children are not confident chopping with a knife, they can roughly grate a peeled onion or carrot instead.

If you need to slice a cake in half to make a layer cake, insert toothpicks at intervals around the cake's circumference halfway down the side. Keep the top steady with one hand, and use a serrated knife to cut just above the toothpicks. Be sure your knife is long enough to cut all the way through the cake.

Don't put knives in a sink filled with water and suds as they can't be seen. Always clean knives immediately and store safely.

wooden tools Keep the wooden spoon you use for cooking savoury dishes separate from the one for sweet dishes. Wood absorbs strong flavours and could spoil your freshly baked cake.

A wooden chopping board will also absorb flavours so use a plastic one when chopping raw or cooked meat, onions and other strong smelling foods.

measuring When you are measuring, make sure you fill the cup to the top of the line you are measuring to — not under or over. When using cups to measure dry ingredients don't put the cup into the ingredient jar to fill it. Spoon the contents from the jar into the cup and level the top with a knife for an accurate measure. In baking it is important to use exactly the right amounts of ingredients.

Measure liquids in a special measuring jug. Measure dry ingredients, such as flour and cocoa powder, in measuring cups. When you pour a liquid into a container it flows into every crevice, but something such as sugar or flour won't settle perfectly and so needs a wide container to settle compactly. If you use a measuring jug for your dry ingredients you'll be adding more than the recipe requires.

sifting Sift dry ingredients, such as flour and cocoa powder, to remove any lumps before you add them to mixing bowls.

eggs To separate egg whites and yolks use either a plastic egg separator (available from the supermarket) or try the plate method. Crack an egg onto a small plate and place a glass over the yolk. Tilt the plate towards the bowl and allow the white of the egg to run into the bowl while you hold the yolk with the glass.

Even a speck of egg yolk can prevent egg whites from being beaten into a stiff foamy mixture. So, if a little bit of yolk does escape into your egg whites scoop it out

147

with the eggshell. A jagged edge is handy for picking up little specks of yolk.

If a recipe calls for either egg whites or egg yolks, don't throw away the part of the egg the recipe doesn't require, instead use it in another recipe. For example, pavlova requires egg whites and custard uses egg yolks. Egg yolks will keep for a couple of days in the fridge if you cover them with a little water and seal them in an airtight container.

timers When you are cooking, set a timer. Make sure it is loud enough to hear even if you are in the bottom of the garden — or better still, take it with you.

testing cakes Use a metal or wooden skewer to poke into the middle of a cake to see if it is cooked. If the skewer comes out clean, then the cake is cooked. If the skewer comes out with wet mixture on it, the cake needs more cooking time.

safety When children are ready, teach them safety basics such as to lift the back of the lid off a hot saucepan first so the steam escapes away from their faces.

handling hot dishes Always use oven mitts when taking things out of the oven but make sure they fit properly to avoid accidents.

If you use wet tea towels to remove hot baking dishes from the oven, the heat will go straight through the tea towel and give you a nasty burn.

cooling You can blow on liquids such as thin soups, tea or coffee to cool them, but for thick liquids the best method for cooling is to rapidly stir and scoop.

Before icing a cake or cupcakes, make sure the cake is cold. If it is warm the icing or cream will run off.

chilling While cooking with kids is lots of fun, rewarding for all those involved and may even put dinner on the table, you might well feel like a drink after it is all over. In your devotion to the task at hand you may have forgotten to put that bottle of wine or beer into the fridge, so here is a guide to chilling your required refreshment.

* A warm bottle of wine cools to 10°C (50°F) in about two hours in the refrigerator, 45 minutes in the freezer or 20 minutes in an ice bucket full of ice.

* To chill a bottle of beer takes three hours in the refrigerator or 25 minutes in an ice bucket full of ice. Avoid the freezer as beer bottles may crack.

cleaning Clean up as you go because it is safer, tidier and makes cooking a whole lot easier if you don't have to fossick through a mess to look for tools or ingredients.

the real thing If you discover your children have a passion for cooking, take them to the source so they can understand the skill involved in producing authentic, quality products. Each state in Australia has plenty of producers making cheese, chocolate, breads, cakes, pasta and icecream among other delicious food.

conversion chart

oven temperatures

VERY LOW	120°C	250°F
LOW	150°C	300°F
MOD. LOW	160°C	325°F
MODERATE	180°C	350°F
MOD. HOT	190°C	375°F
HOT	200°C	400°F
VERY HOT	230°C	450°F

dry ingredients

15 g	½ oz	300 g	10 oz
30 g	1 oz	350 g	12 oz
45 g	1½ oz	375 g	13 oz
60 g	2 oz	400 g	14 oz
75 g	2½ oz	425 g	15 oz
100 g	3½ oz	440 g	15½ oz
115 g	4 oz	470 g	16½ oz
140 g	5 oz	500 g	1 lb 1 oz (17 oz)
170 g	6 oz	750 g	1½ lb
200 g	7 oz	1 kg	2 lb 3 oz
250 g	9 oz		

liquids

30 ml	1 fl oz	300 ml	10 fl oz
60 ml	2 fl oz	375 ml	13 fl oz
100 ml	3½ fl oz	410 ml	14 fl oz
125 ml	4½ fl oz(½ cup)	470 ml	16½ fl oz
155 ml	5½ fl oz	500 ml	17½ fl oz (2 cups)
170 ml	6 fl oz (⅔ cup)	600 ml	1 pint
200 ml	7 fl oz	750 ml	24 fl oz (3 cups)
250 ml	8½ fl oz(1 cup)	1 litre	2 pints (4 cups)

cup and spoon measures

1 cup	250 ml/8 fl oz	1 tablespoon	20 ml
½ cup	125 ml/4 fl oz	1 teaspoon	5 ml
⅓ cup	80 ml/2½ fl oz	½ teaspoon	2.5 ml
¼ cup	60 ml/2 fl oz	¼ teaspoon	1.25 ml

length

5 mm	¼ inch	15 cm	6 inches
1 cm	½ inch	20 cm	8 inches
2 cm	¾ inch	25 cm	10 inches
5 cm	2 inches	30 cm	12 inches
8 cm	3¼ inches	45 cm	18 inches
10 cm	4 inches	50 cm	20 inches
12 cm	5 inches	61 cm	24 inches

151

books to read

The Very Hungry Caterpillar *Eric Carle, Penguin, 1994*
This is a great book for preschoolers with its interactive pages
and positive message about healthy eating. Guaranteed to
become a much-loved favourite.

Cool Kids Cook *Donna Hay, Murdoch Books, 2000, Australia*
Donna Hay's philosophy about kids and cooking is 'make it real'.
Her well-designed cooking book for kids is a rarity because it
doesn't patronise them and includes simple, delicious recipes that
can be used every day, rather than just for desserts or baking.

Roald Dahl's Revolting Recipes *and* **Even More Revolting
Recipes** *Random House Children's Books, 1996*
Not the most appetising collection of recipes but sure to
intrigue Roald Dahl fans as all the recipes are based on food
and drinks featured in his weird and wonderful books.

How to Teach Kids to Cook *Gabriel Gate, Allen & Unwin,
2002, Australia*
With its 60-plus recipes, and lots of inside information from a
well-known cook, this book will help kids become self-assured
long before they have a chance to outgrow it.

parties

Apart from trying to get your child into a selective school, throwing them a single-digit-birthday party could be the most stressful pastime for parents these days. Having been at daycare for three years, Lucy has brought home up to twenty lolly bags in her time. She's been invited to McDonald's (a few times), the fairy shop (lots), the movies (once), and the park (regularly). But never have we been invited into a home.

Parties used to be about having friends come over to see your room with all its hidden treasures. Well, for girls, anyway. For boys — and here I am living vicariously through 11-year-old Monte — it seems a birthday party is the perfect excuse for having friends over to walk the streets of the neighbourhood. But if the day is all about making the birthday girl or boy feel ultra special, why is it so common to attend a party where the venue or entertainment becomes centre stage?

Our friend Rachel threw one of the best birthdays Lucy has been to. Our children are a year apart and this particular summer it was Odessa's third birthday. Lucy's invitation said she needed her swimmers, but the party wasn't at the beach — and I knew Rachel and Adam didn't have a pool. So I rang to find out what was going on. 'Just turn up on the day and make sure Lucy has her costume,' was all Rachel would tell me. So we did … and got such a surprise. The look on Lucy's face said it all. In the back garden were six borrowed paddling pools of different shapes and sizes, all pushed up against one another, to resemble a shallow plastic olympic pool. There were toys in each one, pouring cups, animals, boats and Barbies. The children, as they walked down the drive, looked as if they had just entered Willy Wonka's Chocolate Factory. Give a child something they truly love and they will melt. Give it to them six times over and they won't be able to speak.

I was reminded of Odessa's party a few weeks ago when Lucy brought home two invitations from kindy friends for parties on consecutive weekends. Both were at the same fairy store, which Lucy had been to before, so there wasn't a flicker of anticipation in her eyes: she knew what she was in for. And given the venue, performance and treats are repeated at each party, Lucy can never remember whose was whose.

If Odessa's is Lucy's most memorable birthday party, then Monte's has to be Daniel's grass-sliding party. Daniel is one of four siblings, a rarity in our modern world, and only one of his parents works so their lives are full of creative solutions. Daniel and Monte are at school together and live only a couple of streets apart. Nearby is a huge park with playing fields and a steep grass embankment. Daniel's seventh birthday party invitation requested Monte to arrive at 2 pm (clever move, no need to supply lunch), and byo (bring your own) huge piece of cardboard. About eight boys were invited and all spent a wonderful afternoon sliding down the grassy embankment on their cardboard. They took a break after an hour for cake and a few cans of soft drink, but really all they wanted to do was slide. We offered to stay but there was no need. Little supervision was required because the boys weren't interested in anything but racing each other down the hill.

Contrast that with a girlfriend's experience. Her daughter had a new daycare friend and both mother and daughter had been talking all week about going to her party. I don't know who was more excited — my friend or her daughter. She wanted to see how the mother would throw a party for a pre-schooler in an apartment that had been featured in an exquisite design/architecture magazine. But I don't think she was prepared for what she saw.

Stepping out of the lift and clicking her way across the parquet floors of the apartment's entrance revealed little — it was when she walked past the balcony (or 'terrace' as the host referred to it) that she realised things had gone too far in the competitive world of children's parties. Their king-sized bed had been taken from the main bedroom to make room for the hired jumping castle. The bed was leaning against the balcony wall. And that, sadly, is the truth.

I have also fallen into the trap of thinking money makes a party easier and better, and therefore more memorable. Our mistaken effort was what we affectionately refer to as 'Lucy's bad fairy party'. She was turning three and fully immersed in everything fairy. Keen to have the party at home, we went searching for a fairy to invite. For $150 the Forest Fairy said she was free to fly over for an hour or so. We liked the Forest Fairy because animals were part of her performance.

'Great, we've got chickens and guinea pigs if you need them.' When she didn't reply I assumed she was busy with creative thinking.

We told Lucy a 'real live fairy' would be flying from the forest to her birthday party, and again she couldn't speak, such was the anticipation. The big day arrived and as each little friend came to the front door, Lucy grabbed hold of them and pulled one of those faces that says I am going to burst: 'A fairy is coming, a real live fairy,' she squealed. All the fairy princesses by now had arrived, so all we were waiting for was the Forest Fairy Queen. Half an hour past the time she was due my mobile phone rang. The Forest Fairy had been through some boyfriend trouble the night before, got loot and was now running late. Too much information, really, but I was thankful she was coming because I don't know how I would have ever explained it to all the little girls if she hadn't.

In she walked laden with bags and the biggest CD player I have seen, but in no Forest Fairy mood. I was expecting her to sneak in, squirrel away her tools of the trade and 'fly' down to the garden where all her little fairies were waiting. But she didn't. She huffed and puffed and talked too much. She was also the most uncomfortable adult I have ever seen in the company of children, who are normally very forgiving, but were looking worried. Each time she asked them to sit, stand or turn they would look to me as if to ask, should we?

It was getting so embarrassing I had no choice but to jump in and start playing games while the Forest Fairy stood by with a look of such gratitude I started to feel sorry for her. That is, until she switched to a face full of horror. I had announced it was time for a treasure hunt and that all the little fairies should come inside and get a paper bag for collecting treasure. I was talking to the children but looking straight at the Forest Fairy because this was her cue to hide the lollies she had brought along as part of our agreement (there must have been *something* in all those bags of hers that related to Lucy's party). But the look on her face told me differently.

After all the kids had been picked up, Roberto poured drinks for the friends who were left and we flopped onto the lounge to shake our heads and dissect the life of the world's worst Forest Fairy.

If it hadn't been for Lisa, who had quickly driven to the local shop and brought back a box of chocolates, the children would have been collecting fruit for their treasure hunt. And luckily we had a packet of muesli bars in the cupboard otherwise there would have been no prizes to give out to our little guests. And she had no plans for the chickens or guinea pigs. In fact, I don't think she had a plan whatsoever. We finally kicked her out when, during the singing of happy birthday, she started passing out pieces of paper for the children to colour in. The party was so bad it became funny. And, yes, we paid her.

So what is it with kids and their birthday parties? What happened to a few friends coming over, playing a couple of simple games and eating too much fairy bread? When did parents decide to hijack the process? Birthdays are for remembering the day you were born, to mark another year passed and to acknowledge you exist. Sure, it's meant to be a special day, but whoever said it had to cost a lot, in money and exhaustion?

Perhaps it all starts with the first birthday. You spotlessly clean the house, your friends remark on what a fabulous domestic god and goddess you are, while their babies spend the morning giving you something to do once everyone has gone. Maybe it would be a lot simpler to admit year one is all about the parents, then you wouldn't feel so overwhelmed by having to provide fairy bread as well as unleavened sourdough. It's exciting, a lot of effort goes in to it and you have no time to speak to anyone. From then on it's no wonder there seem to be only two options: outsource or skip it.

Monte received his first invitation to a McDonald's party in kindergarten. Having worked at McDonald's when I was a kid, I had 'run' a few birthdays in my time. But all I ever did was hand out cold food to large groups and throw away enough for another party. Monte's party turned out to be a drop-off scenario (a last minute change because 40 children had been invited and they couldn't fit the parents in). With hope in our hearts that Monte would still be there an hour later, we left McDonald's and wandered the windy streets of the junction. Safely collected, all he could remember was that he got into trouble for pushing another kid off his chair.

Lucy was just two when she received her first McDonald's invitation. So we battled the windy junction again and with the birthday present safely tucked away, walked up to the second floor of McDonald's. It was pure bedlam. There were so many kids we couldn't even get close to the party girl, so hung back waiting for the McDonald's crew member to do some sorting. But there were far too many of us to fit into We're Going To Have Lots Of Fun Land, so we had to settle for Everyday Land, where Roberto and I sat and watched the kids eat cold chips. They always leave the burgers.

Both Monte and Lucy were born in March, so there is a cashflow problem in our house come March. Monte's last outsourced birthday was his seventh, a swimming party at Homebush Bay Olympic Pool. I was about to give birth to Lucy, so with Roberto and his mum and dad, we took two cars and six boys for lunch and pool games. We spent two hours walking around the various different-shaped pools making sure no one was drowning.

I came home that night and vowed I would never do that again. I would much prefer to take Monte and a couple of friends to the pool for an afternoon that wasn't his birthday. Attach birthday to an outing and suddenly dozens of people have to come, and that's when it gets expensive.

Lucy recently turned four and Monte 11, and both birthdays were grassroot affairs. Monte had his party at Roberto's parents' house because they have a pool and five acres. He wanted to keep it just family because he was having his friends to his Dad's house the following weekend, so we drove up the night before for a sleepover. Lucy and I got up early the next morning and made Monte his requested marble cake. With barbecued hamburgers on the menu, there was little else to do other than slice tomatoes, beetroots and lettuce. It was a great day and very relaxed. The kids played in the pool and Roberto's brothers came with their families, as did our much-loved neighbours, Greg and Jo. Very simple. Very special.

And then it was Lucy's turn. Eight friends were invited to our house for a couple of hours on a Saturday morning. One was from kindy, Holly, and the rest were children of our friends. I planned a few games, thinking the kids would enjoy being organised, but halfway through realised they were a wee bit small for that. We played pass the castle (most people would call this 'pass the parcel') and musical hats, a take on musical chairs. To play it, have the kids form a circle and if there are eight kids place seven hats in the middle. When the music starts the kids walk around the circle, and when the music stops they scramble for a hat to put on. The hatless child, and one hat, then move out of the circle. It seemed like a great idea, except I didn't account for how particular four-year-olds are about shape and colour. They were never going to scramble for just any old hat.

Next up was the egg and spoon race. But this didn't work well, either. No matter how many times I showed the kids how to hold the spoon handle with one hand, while balancing the egg, they preferred to use two hands or to cup the spoon in their palm. And that was the end of my repertoire, so the kids all made for Lucy's room and happily demolished it over the next hour.

Kids want in parties, I have come to realise, what they want in their dinners. Repetition is not necessarily a bad thing, as long as the child feels special. That is why a party at home can work year after year whereas the back room of a fairy shop won't necessarily make it into their top ten all-time favourites. Their home is *their* home, which means only their party will ever be held there. As long as the games and guest list are updated each year you could recycle the same party year after year because all kids really want from their birthday is to feel thoroughly loved and special. Now how easy is that.

prepare to party

essentials **Absolutely top of your to-do list for party day:**

* **make sure your child feels extra special**
* **ensure all his or her good friends have been invited**
* **leave a few surprises for the birthday boy or girl, too**

best friends **If your child has a best friend, make sure they can come on the date you are planning for the party before you go ahead with bookings and invitations. The day just won't be the same for them without their partner in crime by their side.**

involve the birthday girl or boy **If your child is old enough, sit down with him or her and offer a few suggestions for the theme and structure of the party, and let them choose which one they would like. Don't ask your child to come up with the party plan because disappointment may follow.**

162

invitations Send out invitations at least three weeks ahead of time.

plan Plan what you are going to do, eat, play and give to each child when they leave. Start collecting party paraphernalia a couple of weeks prior to the big day and throw it all into a plastic tub so it's easy to access when party time arrives.

timing Weekend parties are better for younger children, while older children will enjoy an after-school party, if you can manage it. They love spending all day together in anticipation of going home together.

venue Home parties are generally less expensive than hired venues and you are free to make the party whatever time suits your family.

present opening Do you or don't you open presents with your party guests? Opening presents after everyone has gone home is much less stressful (there is no one to hear your child announce he or she doesn't like the present) and you are less likely to lose bits and pieces if you are on hand. It is also a wonderful way to end a day that may well have been filled with both laughter and tears. If you open presents after everyone has left, it's nice to send thank you notes (you can write them with your child if they are too young to do it themselves). Ask them to tell you why they loved each gift and include it in your note. Some editing may be required.

numbers **Big is not always best. Remember:**

* **the number of guests should be the age of your child plus one. However, this rule probably doesn't apply until your child is at least three.**
* **If you are planning games make sure you invite an even number of children so no one is left out.**
* **Older children handle bigger groups better than younger children.**

party food

We have come a long way with children's party food. A recipe written in the early 1970s requires pineapple rings to be placed on each plate and half a banana stuck standing in the middle. Finally, a glacé cherry is to be ceremoniously perched on the top, secured with a toothpick. Another, that I've thankfully never come across in real life, asks you to cut four hard-boiled eggs in half and scoop out the yolks. Place the yolks, mayonnaise, crushed potato chips and one rasher of cooked, chopped bacon into a bowl and mix together before spooning back into the egg halves. Recovering a lost art does not mean you have to take everything it has to offer.

SAUSAGE SIZZLE If you have a barbecue at home, then a sausage sizzle is the easiest way to feed everyone. Have lots of bread rolls and sliced-white already buttered and serve the sausages on a plate. Whoever is hungry can make their own sausage roll, or sandwich, with or without sauce and barbecued onions. Of course you have to have fairy bread, lollies and chips, but that doesn't mean you can't have a fruit platter, too.

LUNCH BAGS If you know you are only having children to your party, you can prepare each a lunch bag with lots of surprises inside: a sandwich, small packet of chips, chocolate bar, small juice, a small bag of popcorn and a cheesestick, for example. You can be guaranteed the room will be quiet for at least 15 minutes as the kids fossick about in their bags. This is especially exciting for four-year-olds who are off to school the following year and can't wait to have a lunch bag of their own. Make it special by drawing each guest's name on a bag and decorating them. The birthday boy or girl can help do this in preparation for the party.

SAUSAGE ROLLS AND SANDWICHES If you have the time, and energy, you can make homemade sausage rolls filled with minced beef and vegetables, or cheese or vegemite sandwiches cut out with a large cookie cutter, perhaps in shapes of letters, stars or circles. Avoid serving peanut butter because it can cause allergic reactions in some children.

MEATBALLS AND NACHOS Meatballs are another worthy contender for a kids' party, but keep the sweet chilli sauce dipping bowl well away from the regular tomato sauce so there is no confusion. Nachos is another favourite with kids (make sure you let it cool so the hot, melted cheese does not burn their mouths).

165

SWEET THINGS And although you will be having cake later, you can always serve freshly made scones with jam and cream, chocolate crackles or coconut ice before blowing out the candles.

CAKE So what about the cake? There is always the store-bought version, but it's lots of fun to make your own. If you are confident your homemade attempt will turn out as planned, then there are endless possibilities, and if you're not, do a practice run the weekend before. It certainly won't go to waste.

Marble cakes are well-loved. To ice, just drizzle pink or blue icing over the top. If your icing is made without butter — and includes only icing sugar, a little water and food colouring — it will harden with a glossy finish as it drips down the sides.

Or you can bake enough cupcakes for everyone and top them with a buttery vanilla icing. Place a daisy on top of each one and assemble them in ever-increasing circles so they look like one big cake.

party games

I have included games and ideas for children's parties up to 11 years old, however they work best for those aged between four and seven. Children of this age arrive, need no introductions, but love to be told what to do and what is going to happen next. A group of older kids prefers doing things their way and in their own time, as long as you supply the food and drinks (and maybe lifts home for everyone).

three- to five-year-olds

MUSICAL HATS If you are having an outdoor party you can play musical hats instead of musical chairs.

Have the children form a circle and place a jumble of hats in the middle, one fewer than the number of children playing. The funnier the hats the better. When the music starts they trot around clockwise and when the music stops each must grab a hat and put it on though somebody will be left hatless. The hatless one, plus one hat, withdraws from the game after each round until there is a winner.

THE FARMYARD An adult makes up an amusing story about the farmyard, bringing in funny names of various animals and birds such as 'cheeky chicken' or 'Harry Horse'. The children are each given farmyard names and as the storyteller mentions these names in the story, the players must stand up and make the sound of the animals they represent. Every time the storyteller mentions 'the farmyard', it is a signal for all the players to make their noises simultaneously and triumphantly.

PASS THE PARCEL This is an old favourite. Wrap a small gift in a large parcel, using many separate sheets of different coloured paper, each tied up with string or secured with sticky tape. Remember the colour of the last piece of paper if you want the birthday girl or boy to be the one to open it. Players are seated in a circle and the parcel is passed around to music. The player who has the parcel when the music stops must unwrap one

167

layer only and then pass the parcel on when the music recommences. The player who takes off the last piece of wrapping to find a gift is the winner. A small treat can also be placed in between each layer, such as a chocolate or lolly.

VARIATIONS ON PASS THE PARCEL Within each wrapping include a note with an instruction, such as hop on one leg, run around the circle, do a somersault, clap hands, pretend to cry, laugh, or pat the head of the person sitting next to you. The last layer hides a box filled with a small treat for everyone which the birthday boy or girl can hand out.

I HAVE A LITTLE DOG The children sit in a circle on the floor. One player with a handkerchief in his or her hand walks around the outside of the ring, saying, 'I have a little dog but he won't bite you, but he won't bite you, but he won't bite you, but he *will* bite you!' She or he then drops the handkerchief into the lap of the chosen player and runs off around the ring. The child with the handkerchief has to jump up and try to catch them before they can run around the ring to the vacant place and sit down. If they don't catch up, it is their turn to walk around the outside of the ring singing 'I have a little dog …'.

BUNNY HUNT The children are asked to crouch and hop around imitating rabbits. When a parent calls out 'Hunter' the children must immediately stop still. Those who fall over or wobble are out of the game. Then the parent calls out 'Hunter's gone' and the children begin hopping again. Award a small prize to the last child still hopping.

MATCHING GAME Give each child a paper bag with six items inside. They may include such items as a paper clip, hair band, playing card, five-cent coin, pen, pencil, teaspoon, etc. Each bag must have different items inside. Then send the children on a treasure hunt around the room to find the objects that match the ones in their bag.

SIMON SAYS Ask the party guests to stand in a line, with an adult out in front. Starting with the words 'Simon Says' the adult gives instructions such as 'Simon Says hands on your head', 'Simon says hands on your knees', 'Simon says wriggle your fingers'. The children follow the instructions. But when the adult gives an instruction that does not begin with 'Simon Says', those who respond to that instruction are out of the game.

six- to seven-year-olds

BLINDMAN'S BLUFF Blindfold one child and stand him or her in the centre of the other children who have formed a circle. The children move around him or her until he or she tells them to stop and then points. The child nearest to his or her pointing moves into the circle and is chased until he or she is caught by the 'blindman' who is still wearing the blindfold. Once the 'blindman' has caught the child he or she has to identify the child, still wearing the blindfold. If he or she is right, the child who has been caught becomes the 'blindman', if not, the original player tries again.

169

CHINESE WHISPERS Sit everybody in a circle. An adult whispers something to the child sitting next to them, who then whispers it to the next child and so on until the last child says aloud what has just been whispered to him or her. The adult then reveals what the original whisper was, which usually makes everyone laugh because it is so different from the final whisper.

THOUGHT ANIMALS One player starts off by saying 'I am thinking of an animal' and begins to describe it. Each player has to guess what the animal is before anybody else does, but if he or she calls out the wrong answer there is no second try for them in that round. The first person to guess correctly is given a lolly or treat and it becomes their turn to say 'I am thinking of an animal' and describe the animal. Once a person has won a lolly or treat they must be quiet so each person has a chance of winning.

PIÑATA A papier-mâché object filled with lollies that hangs from a tree (or clothes line, fence, etc.). The children have to break open the piñata to get the treats by hitting it with a stick. Piñatas are easy and lots of fun to make because making them involves a messy gooey mixture of flour and water, balloons and crepe paper. Ensure you leave enough time to make your piñata, keeping in mind it will need to dry overnight.

HOW TO MAKE A BASIC PIÑATA Blow up a balloon the size and shape you require. Don't make it too small or it may be hard for the children to strike. Papier-mâché glue is made by combining flour and water in equal parts, but add more flour or water if you need to thicken or thin it. Cut strips of newspaper to about 3 cm

(1½ inches) wide, dip each strip into the gooey flour and water mixture until it is well-coated and then place over the balloon, making sure it is smooth and there are no air bubbles. Repeat until the whole balloon is covered in a single layer of newspaper strips, except the knot (this is where you pull the balloon out once the newspaper has dried and formed a tough shell).

Wrap string around the two fattest parts of the balloon so the string forms a cross at the top of the balloon and four pieces of string hang down and meet together at the bottom, near the knot. Leave about a 20 cm (8 inch) tail and cover the balloon with a second layer of newspaper strips, ensuring the string is completely covered. Balance the balloon on a glass and leave it overnight to dry.

Once it is completely dry, pop the balloon near the knot with a pin. Pull out as much of the balloon as you can but don't worry if some is left inside. With a scalpel blade, cut a small opening in the piñata and fill with lollies and confetti, then securely tape over the hole with masking tape.

You are now ready to decorate your piñata and can make it into anything you like — a fish, a flower, a snake — whatever you or your child come up with, the shape of the original balloon may influence your choice.

Materials for decorating your piñata include different coloured crepe paper, aluminium foil and pieces of felt. Layer the materials for different effects. Pipe cleaners are great for antenna if your piñata is a bug.

eight to ten-year-olds

NAME BINGO This is a good game for a party where the guests may not know each other. Before everyone arrives, find a piece of stiff paper or cardboard for each child, with enough squares drawn for the number of guests. Hand one out to each child, with a slip of paper and pencil. Ask each child to write his or her name on the slip of paper and put it into a bowl. The children then walk around and ask each of the guests what their name is and write it down in a square until they have filled in all the squares. It doesn't matter which names go in which squares, just that all the squares are filled in.

When they have finished ask them to sit in a circle around you. Mix up the slips of paper with the names written on them and pull them out one at a time and read aloud each name. The name's owner stands up and says, 'That's me', then everyone crosses that name off their card. The game could stop there but a more competitive version involves continuing reading until all the names have been called out and somebody has a whole line, vertical or horizontal, crossed out. He or she then stands up and shouts 'Bingo'.

BANG BANG Make two equal rows of chairs, one for each team, and under each chair place a paper bag. Seat the teams on the chairs. On the count of three the first person from each team has to get up and run around the row of chairs back to their seat, grab the paper bag from under their chair, blow it up and burst it with their hand. This is the signal for the next person to follow suit. The team who finishes first wins.

CONSEQUENCES This game is best played if the children are not told what the game is about, but follow instructions for each step.

Sit all the party guests in a circle. Each player is given a piece of paper and pencil and begins by writing an adjective at the top of the paper. Then the paper is folded over at the top, hiding the word, and passed on to the person on the left. Under the fold, on blank paper, the players now write the name of the person sitting to their left, fold the paper over and pass it on again. Next the children write down their favourite place, fold the paper and pass it on. Next, they write a question, fold the paper and pass it on. Now they write the answer to their question, fold the paper over and pass it on. Finally, they are told to write down a consequence, that is, what happened at the meeting place after their question was asked. The pieces of paper are then unfolded and everybody reads aloud what is a very funny story.

party themes

puppet show For three- to six- year olds. Two adults are needed, or an older brother or sister can help. Cut up an old sheet or a piece of material into two even pieces and drape over a broom handle to make the puppet theatre's curtains. The broom can be balanced between two chairs. If you don't have puppets, use dolls or stuffed toys.

Spend some time the week before the party working out your show. Take into account the kids who are coming and incorporate something about each one into your performance, keeping in mind, of course, that the birthday boy or girl has to be the hero of the story.

Use the children's names, streets they live in, what they like doing and anything else your child has told you about their friends. Make it as funny and silly as you can.

Once the show is over, you can help the kids make their own finger puppets to take home. They are simple to make from felting wool (see page 198) and each child can make four, one for each finger. Have bits and pieces for the kids to stick on for eyes and mouths.

By the time you've put on your show, the kids have made their finger puppets and everyone has had something to eat and drink, it will probably be time to finish up. The kids will have had a great time and their finger puppets will remind them of a special party.

ready set cook For seven- to eleven- year olds. Boys and girls will enjoy spending a morning cooking a party lunch. Plan a menu that requires lots of hands-on action so everybody can join in. Threading skewers or rolling out pizza dough, grating cheese for nachos or rolling meatballs are good examples of an action-packed party menu.

Provide everyone with their own apron, which they can take home at the end of the day. Your child may like to spend the weekend prior to their party decorating and personalising one for each of their friends.

Plan the menu together and make a list of all the ingredients you will need. If you don't have time to shop but do have access to the internet, order the supplies from a home shopping website such as Coles, Woolworths or Shopfast. (At time of publication, these services were only available in capital cities.)

As a gift for each child, sift together the dry ingredients for a simple biscuit batter or gingerbread. Seal them in a ziplock bag, ensuring all the air has been pushed out. Place it and the instructions for completing the recipe inside a brightly coloured paper bag along with a cookie cutter. Make one for each child to take home and when they make the biscuits they will remember the wonderful day they had.

knitting

Newspaper journalists know a little about a lot. Every time a story comes your way three things can happen: you have a chance of getting your byline in the newspaper, proving to the editor you still exist; you top up your general knowledge; or, if you are really lucky, and journalism thrives on luck, you might even change the world — or second best, change your own life in some small way.

The third of these is what happened when I arrived at Sydney's Red Cross headquarters one May morning to meet an academic who had written a book on volunteering. I was doing a story for *The Australian* for its '1942 War On Our Doorstep' coverage, acknowledging the sixtieth anniversary of the Japanese push towards Australia. My interest was in the role of volunteering and, as I was a little early, I explored the Red Cross store.

I love hand-knitted jumpers for children and so was in seventh heaven when I saw racks and stacks of pure wool hand-knitted jumpers, all under $40. Something unheard of in stores where they are nearly all acrylic and if you do find a pure wool jumper it usually costs a ridiculous amount. Both Lucy and Monte have hand-knitted jumpers picked up from country markets but in department stores and boutiques, you pay dearly.

I bought a cute little red jumper for $20 from the Red Cross store and while it sat on the table at home waiting for Lucy's friend Giselle to turn three, I happened to look at it closely one afternoon. If I imagine I can change the world, I thought as I smoothed its silky threads, I can surely learn how to knit.

There is nothing that impresses my kids more than showing them you can do something with your hands. Changing the world rates poorly on their radar — it matters little to them that Roberto and I can get up at 7.45 am on a Saturday morning, feed two kids, make poached eggs, ask Monte four times to get his swimming costume, Lucy eight times to find her fairy wings, feed the guinea pigs and chickens, pack the dishwasher, sweep up the beach from the floor, shower, clean teeth, pack a bag for ballet class (to be followed by a fairy party then a surf for Monte), and leave the house at 8.30 am to make the 8.45 am ballet class. Nope, that means zip. But when I sat down in the middle of all that to sew elastic to Lucy's ballet slippers to stop them falling off, the look on my three-year-old daughter's face said it all.

(I used my late grandmother's sewing basket that has moved house with me since I inherited it when I first moved out of home at 17. So many things have been lost during my umpteen moves over the years, I wonder how a sewing basket managed to keep up — especially as I have never shown it the kind of respect it truly deserves. I've only ever touched needles and thread, the sewing equivalent of reading *War and Peace*, via Cliff Notes.)

So when I told Monte I wanted to learn to knit, I immediately had his attention. I'm not sure if he believed me at first but once I convinced him, I had no trouble roping him in. We borrowed a couple of books from the library to see just how hard this knitting caper really was and, while books can be helpful, I found out you can't beat a hands-on lesson. Knitting is all about mathematics, following directions and patterns, but I didn't tell Monte any of this because he is not a big fan of maths. Still, I was surprised I didn't have to spin him a yarn about how rewarding it is to make something yourself — he was genuinely keen, perhaps because he is the kind of guy who loves to make stuff and watch 'The Bill'.

The knitting books sat on our kitchen table for a few weeks and Monte kept asking when we were going to start. Each weekend would come and go, and we would be set to go to a wool shop but suddenly it would be 5 pm — and there isn't a wool shop in our area. So I suggested we wait a couple of weeks until Berry.

An historic town about 200 km south of Sydney, Berry is popular with tourists and its bay-windowed arts and craft stores almost outnumber its pubs and cafes. But this week-long trip was going to be spent at our friends' gorgeous house, reclining on their feather-stuffed day bed, out on the wisteria-covered verandah, happily knitting away under the afternoon sun. Well, for me it was, because I had promised Lucy's Barbie a scarf.

If I have an overwhelming regret about my life it would be that I didn't travel overseas when I was young and without serious responsibilities. Roberto did, for three years, which only deepens my regret. But with two kids, a career and accompanying baggage, it's not an option these days. Every time we sit down to plan a holiday, I start with exotic overseas locations — and we end up a few hundred kilometres north or south of Sydney. Although it doesn't bother me as much now, because I have fallen in love with exploring Australia. Since Lucy turned two we have been squashing too much into the car, arguing over its not being a station wagon, and exploring many beautiful, secluded corners of the east coast.

And so this week it is Berry, so we can enjoy the end of Roberto's outdoor cinema season. It's a week we look forward to every year because it means the difficult, and often frustrating, three-month-long ordeal is over and there are nine fabulously uncomplicated months before it starts up again. As much as I love kicking back and being spontaneous on holidays, I am a planner from way back. This holiday's grand plan, for Monte and me, is to learn to knit. Roberto is going to read and Lucy just picks up from where she left off at home — literally, because most of her toys and dolls come with us, to lie around on the floor waiting to be picked up.

We arrive at the house and unpack the car before forcing the kids back into the car to return to Berry for wool and knitting needles. We find every width, colour and texture of ribbon you could possibly want, cross-stitches galore and quilting sets, but no yarn. It is too late in the afternoon to travel anywhere else, so we head home after agreeing to scour nearby towns for supplies the next day.

After a slow morning we head south and find ourselves in Nowra. We drive along its main streets looking for a wool shop (we really want to believe this old-fashioned stalwart is alive and well, enjoying pride of place next to the bank, milk bar and newsagent), and there is Tanya's Wool Store, right next to the tackle shop — natch.

Monte and I go in.

'We know nothing about knitting but would like to start and were wondering what we should buy,' I say, I guess to Tanya herself.

With hindsight — and wonderful advice from Greta's Handcraft Centre in Sydney's Lindfield and Liz Gemmell's knitting classes upstairs — I can confidently say Tanya wasn't at all interested in welcoming us to the knitting world. I was sold a complicated pattern book and wool which is still sitting in its packaging because I can no more knit a jumper now, a year later, than I could when I first bought the wool. Monte did better with his purchases — a latch-hook rug kit and French knitting doll. He is still making the rug, for Lucy, but I fear we will have to have another baby for it to be appreciated. He has also made metres of braid with the French knitting doll — but no one can work out what it should be used for ... except Lucy, who is sharpening her scissor skills, and successfully cut it all up.

Tanya might have told us that knitting is all about practice and advised us to pick up some needles from St Vincent de Paul, buy one ball of wool and practise until our fingers and hands moulded themselves to the needles. In many ways, mastering knitting is like learning to use chopsticks. Tanya might also have told me it is a lot easier to learn from a person than a book, that there are plenty of knitting classes all over Australia, *and* that wool does come in colours a tad more interesting than fire-engine red or British blue or canary yellow, and all kinds of exquisite threads are available. But she just sold me red wool.

I now feel confident enough to start on a scarf for myself — after Lucy told me Barbie fell in love with the blue one I made her. So I return to Greta's Handcraft Centre and find the most gorgeous wool — blue, brown and black intertwined. There is probably a proper name for it but I don't know what it is, I just know it's soft and that I like it. At $12 a ball it's not cheap but my scarf will be a lot cheaper than the one I am modelling it on — a simple scarf made from the same wool, but for $75. I could make that, I thought to myself when I saw it in a shop. I don't have a pattern but use a simple knit stitch with size 7 mm knitting needles that I have retrieved, with barbecue tongs, from behind the television.

I must have started that scarf five times. The first time I didn't make enough stitches and it was too skinny. Then I had too many stitches and it was too wide. I made lots of mistakes and unravelled and knitted, unravelled and knitted. Finally I got the feel for what I was doing and finished my scarf, which I love, mostly because I made it.

I reckon I could call myself a knitter (now I have knitted a whole scarf, Monte knitted a few stitches here and there but I wasn't very good at letting him have a go). I enjoyed sitting in front of the television after Lucy had gone to bed, clicking away. It was so relaxing, particularly as I find it very hard to just sit. 'Just let me finish this,' I would say to poor Monte, 'and then we can do something together.' — now I have found the perfect something. Our neighbours, who love Lucy and Monte and spend a lot of time with them, are having their first baby.

So Monte and I are going to knit them a baby's blanket. It is the perfect project for us to do together because all it requires is nine squares which we'll join using a mattress stitch and we can share the knitting.

Since confessing my new-found hobby I've discovered a number of my friends are avid knitters. One took knitting up to stop smoking and another does it for relaxation. I recently saw a couple of young women sitting in window seats at Starbucks, with steaming coffees cooling off as they fervently knitted away without so much as a word passing between them. As I walked past I wondered if they were having a bad day, because knitting is perfect therapy for a shitty day. I only wish I had known what to do with my purchases from Tanya's Wool Store that day — I could have saved a fortune in wine.

a basic kit

----

yarn Sold in balls with a label or ball-band giving the following information:

WEIGHT OF THE BALL Described as ply, which is the term for a single strand of spun yarn. Strands are twisted together to make 2 ply, 3 ply, 4 ply, up to 12 ply. When knitting for the first time, it is advisable to use a medium to heavy-weight yarn such as 8 ply that has a plain, smooth finish. You can see the stitches easily and won't split the wool as you knit. More elaborate yarns can be confusing.

FIBRE CONTENT That is, cotton, acrylic, wool or a combination.

RECOMMENDED NEEDLE SIZE It is widely accepted that you don't change the recommended needle size by more than two sizes.

RECOMMENDED GAUGE Following the pattern's gauge is the key to knitting pieces to the correct size. A knitted piece's gauge is the number of stitches to a given width and the number of rows to a given length. Most knitting pattern instructions include a recommended gauge and it is vital you match this gauge exactly otherwise your product will be the wrong size.

THE SHADE OF THE YARN Named and/or numbered, accompanied by a dyelot number. Yarn is dyed in batches, or dyelots, and the colour may vary slightly from one batch to another. Such variations are obvious when the yarn is knitted, so always try to purchase all the yarn for a project at the same time and check that all the balls carry the same dyelot number.

WASHING AND PRESSING INSTRUCTIONS You've just spent weeks knitting a unique piece. Spend a few minutes reading the care instructions to ensure it lasts a lifetime.

needles Pairs of needles come in a range of sizes, from large (15 mm) to fine (2 mm) to suit different weights of yarn. They are also available in different lengths to suit the number of stitches required. Circular needles are available for more complicated knitting.

tools To begin with all you need is: a tape measure, a pair of small sharp scissors, yarn needles (which should have large eyes and blunt tips to prevent splitting strands of yarn) and a row counter (to keep count of how many rows you have completed).

optional extras There are many knitting accessories you can buy, such as stitch holders (used for temporarily holding stitches) or ring markers (to mark a particular stitch or row). A needle gauge is handy to determine the size of needles if you buy them from secondhand stores and their size is not indicated.

knitting stitches

There are two fundamental stitches in knitting: knit and purl. It's how you combine these two stitches that changes the look and feel of your finished piece. It's worth knitting small square samples using each stitch for reference for future projects.

GARTER Knit every row.

STOCKINETTE Knit one row, purl the next.

SEED Knit one stitch, purl the next, repeat across the row (cast on an uneven number of stitches).

QUAKER RIDGE Knit two rows, purl two rows; repeat.

KNIT 1, PURL 1 RIBBING Knit one stitch, purl the next; repeat across the row (cast on an even number of stitches).

KNIT 2, PURL 2 RIBBING Knit two stitches, purl two stitches; repeat across row (cast on an even number of stitches).

getting started

making a slip knot The first thing you have to do before you start knitting is make a slip knot. Follow the diagram at left, pulling the piece of wool that is under the needle, through the loop and tighten.

casting on Before knitting you need to create a foundation row — this is called casting on.

1   With the slipknot on the left needle, hold the needle in your left hand, the short yarn-end held firmly under your fingers.

2   Take the other needle in your right hand and insert the tip from left to right into the slipknot, beneath the left needle.

3   With your right hand, wrap yarn behind the point of the right needle (anticlockwise) and bring the yarn forward between the two needles and hook the newly formed loop onto the left needle. >

187

4 Insert the right needle between the two stitches on the left needle. With your right hand wrap yarn behind the point of the right needle (anticlockwise).

5 Bring the looped yarn forward between the two stitches.

6 Hook the loop over the left needle. Repeat until you have cast on the required number of stitches. Before knitting your first row, arrange the stitches so they create a neat ridge at the bottom of the needle.

how to knit

Once they've learnt, nobody ever forgets how to knit. Once you've cast on there will be no holding you back. But before you rush ahead begin by practising: cast on 20 stitches and knit 20 rows. Always position the yarn behind the needles and hold the needle with the cast-on stitches in your left hand, making sure the first stitch is about 2.5 cm (1 inch) from the tip.

1 With your right hand hold the empty needle as you would a knife and insert it into the first stitch, keeping the right needle behind the left.

2 With your right forefinger, wrap the yarn, anticlockwise, behind the point of the right needle and then forward between both needles.

3 Tip the right needle downward, catching this wrapped piece of yarn and drawing it down through the loop on the left needle, creating a large loop on the right needle.

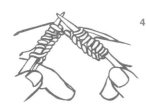

4 Slide the original stitch off the point of the left needle so the stitch is now on the right needle. Gently tug to tighten but be careful not to make your stitches too tight. After every few stitches, push the stitches on the right needle away from the tip to prevent stretching them. Repeat the steps until the left needle is empty. Transfer the needle with the stitches to the left hand and begin the next row.

From *Knitting Basics*

189

how to purl

A purl stitch is made the opposite way to a knit stitch. Practise the purl stitch by casting on about 20 stitches.

1   Hold the needle with the stitches in your left hand. Hold the yarn in front of the empty right needle and insert the right needle into the first stitch on the left needle, from right to left, making sure you keep the right needle in front of the left. With your right forefinger, wrap the yarn anticlockwise around the right needle tip.

2   Lift the right needle upward, catching the wrapped yarn and drawing it through the stitch on the left needle to create a loop on the right needle. 'Slip the original stitch off the left needle. The newly made stitch is now on your right needle.' Repeat steps until the left needle is empty.

3   Now, notice how the purl stitches form a row of 'purl bumps' on the side of the work facing you. 'If you purl several rows, the appearance of the work will be the same as for garter stitch (where all the rows are made up of knit stitches).'

From *Knitting Basics*

joining

It is simple to join another ball of wool, in either the same or a different colour, to your knitting.

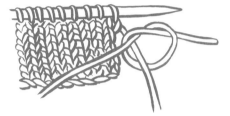
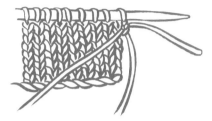

1 Tie the new wool to the exisiting wool, leaving a 10 cm tail.

2 Once finished knitting, weave the tail of the the wool into your work.

casting off

Casting off or binding off links stitches that are no longer required, stopping them from unravelling. You can cast off a whole row or part of a row if required, such as when shaping an armhole. Be careful not to make your casting off too tight or too loose. It should stretch by about the same amount as the rest of the knitted piece. If a more elastic edge is required, for example on an opening, use a needle one or two sizes larger than the previous row.

1 'Knit the first two stitches on the left needle in the usual way onto the right needle. Insert the tip of the left needle, from left to right, through the front of the first stitch on the right needle (the stitch farthest to the right).'

191

2 'Lift the first stitch over the second stitch and off the right needle. One stitch remains on the right needle and one has been cast off.'

3 Knit the next stitch so there are two stitches on the right needle. Repeat above steps as many times as required to cast off required number of stitches. When all stitches have been cast off you should end with one stitch on the right needle. 'Cut the yarn leaving a tail of around 15 cm (6 inches).'

4 'Wrap the tail around the right needle. Lift the last stitch on the right needle over the loop and pull the tail through the last stitch to make a neat finish. The tail may be run in later along a seam or a longer tail may be left and used for sewing a seam.'

From *Knitting Basics*

blocking

Blocking smooths the stitches of your knitting and gives it a finished look. There are two ways to block your knitting, so always refer to the instructions on the ball bands which recommend the best way to block your work.

If you can't use an iron on the yarn you have used, lightly dampen the piece with water and pat it gently with your hands to help the moisture penetrate the fibres. Lay the piece flat, and use your hands to smooth and shape it into place. Pin it to a piece of board covered in cotton fabric and allow to dry flat.

If your yarn can be ironed, lay a piece of clean, dry cloth over your knitting. Gently hold the iron on a low heat, lightly on the surface for a few seconds but don't press or run the iron over the knitting. Repeat until the whole piece has been gently steamed, avoiding the ribbing as pressing it will reduce its elasticity. Keep the garment pinned in shape to the ironing board until it has completely dried.   From *Knitting Basics*

checking your gauge

Knitters vary in how tightly or loosely they knit. These differences affect the finished size of the piece. *Martha Stewart* magazine writes: 'Checking the gauge ensures that the finished [square] has the correct dimensions. After knitting a few [centimetres], lay the [square] flat and measure the width. If it's smaller than desired, according to the gauge on the pattern, start over and work with a pair of needles one size larger. If it's larger than desired, start over and work with a pair of needles one size smaller.'

knitting tricks

knit evenly **Try to knit evenly, keeping stitches loose enough so you can fit a needle in easily.**

uneven stitches **If your stitches look uneven form them close to the tips. The stitch you are knitting into (on the left needle) should be no more than 2.5 cm (1 inch) from the tip, depending on needle size and yarn weight.**

193

reusing wool **If you need to unravel your wool to start again, roll it into a ball over steam to stop it going crinkly.**

purling **When you purl a stitch, remember to put your needle into the stitch from back to front, or right to left, making sure it is in front of the left needle.**

using your thumb **Use your left-hand thumb (if you are right-handed) not your forefinger when pushing stitches from the left needle to the right needle. Your little finger won't cramp this way.**

count stitches **Remember to count your stitches at the end of each row to make sure you haven't dropped or added any.**

baby's blanket

Materials: 8 ply yarn, approximately 850 m (I used five balls of 'Sirdar Snowflake', a polyester that, once knitted, looks and feels like terry towelling), and size 8 knitting needles.

Nine squares will make a baby's blanket, but it's up to you how many squares you make, depending on how big you want your blanket to be. For each square cast on 35 stitches, knit 30 cm (12 inches) then cast off. The smaller the stitches the warmer the blanket will be.

Martha Stewart magazine, published in the US, suggests applying a decorative trim to the squares by using a blanket stitch in a contrasting yarn. 'Thread a blunt yarn needle with lightweight yarn, insert needle from back to front through edge of lower left corner. Insert needle into knitted fabric at top right of first stitch. Bring out at edge, keeping the yarn loop under the needle. Continue stitching, working from left to right until all sides are edged.'

To finish, use mattress stitch to sew together the squares in rows of three, then sew the rows together. To begin, place two squares side by side, right side up. Thread yarn needle with the same yarn used for knitting and sew together. If your squares have decorative blanket-stitch borders, avoid sewing over the borders of coloured thread by inserting the yarn needle under the threads of the blanket stitch, into the edge of the fabric. For a stretchy seam, keep your sewing fairly loose. Weave in the loose ends through the back of several stitches, picking up the surface loops only. Finish by blocking.

felting

Felting is fluffy fun. Simply dampen felting wool with hot soapy water and work the fibres into any shape you like. It's not complicated (children as young as three will enjoy the mess, process and finished product) but needs a little time and patience.

Felting wool is different from knitting wool. It is available in lots of bright colours and comes pre-washed and carded (brushed straight). It looks a little like long strands of cotton wool, but each strand has microscopic shingles or scales that overlap. When the wool is dampened the shingles stretch and swell, catching each other before springing back, locking together. The more you work the wool the more it tightens. As it dries, the wool becomes dense felt.

method and equipment

A BOWL OF SOAPY WATER Mix four tablespoons of liquid detergent, free of scents and dyes, to six cups of water, or use pure laundry soap — make a jelly by combining two cakes with eight cups of water, then add half a cup of your jelly mixture to four cups of hot water.)

BAMBOO PLACEMAT for felting handles.

SPONGE AND BAKING TRAY to catch excess water.

WEIGHING SCALES if you want to make more than one of the same object. This ensures you will use the same amount of wool for each.

A DRAINING BOARD to full the felt. By using hot and cold water the wool thickens while the fibres shrink into a firm material. As you rub it back and forth across the draining board's ridges the felt shrinks in the direction you are rubbing, so make sure you change directions to ensure an even finish.

making a felt ball This is the simplest of felt projects. You just wind strands of wool into a ball, dunk it in water and shape it.

You can put small bells, split peas or tiny stones inside the ball, but make sure to wrap them in cling wrap first to keep them dry and stop the wool from clogging them.

Start with a small ball of fleece and keep adding floooo until you have the size you want. Soak the ball in hot water and gently roll it from hand to hand. Keep doing this for 10 minutes, dipping it back into the hot soapy water as it cools. The wool may look a mess but don't worry, it will harden.

You can decorate the ball by winding strips of contrasting colours, in intervals, around the ball, or sticking circle scrolls dipped in the soapy water to the outside of your ball. After you have finished decorating, dip your ball into the hot soapy water again, rinse and let dry.

You can make a necklace or bracelet from felt beads by poking a toothpick through each one just before your small bead balls have dried. Using a piece of wool, thread the beads, making sure you tie a knot at each end of the beads so they stay spaced out.

finger puppets Wrap fleece around the pointer finger you don't use for writing. The wool should be snug but not tight. Keep adding wool until you can't feel your knuckle any more. Dip your woolly finger into the soapy water and, using your other fingertips, press the puppet into shape. Keep dipping and pressing until the fibres hold together. Add stripes or spots to decorate it, just as you did with your ball.

Harden the felt by rubbing it, still on your finger, along the ridges of the draining board. Keep changing direction and be careful you don't rub too hard. Rinse with warm water and let dry.

Glue on eyes, ears, manes, hair or beaks by cutting shapes from store-bought felt (you will need a lot of glue because felt is ultra absorbent). You can also make eyes with buttons or thread.

books to read

Knitting Basics: All you need to know to take up your needles and get knitting *Betty Barnden, Quarto Publishing, London, 2002*

This is a great book for the knitting novice. Its diagrams and instructions are clear and easy to follow. I refer to it regularly whenever I get into trouble and it always answers my questions.

Kids Knitting *Melanie D Falick, Artisan, 1998*

I found this book on www.amazon.com and while I haven't read it, it looks like the junior edition of Barnden's *Knitting Basics*. One review says it is suitable for children from four years old too: 'Not only are projects and skills arranged in an orderly progression of difficulty, but the directions also begin explicitly and gradually move toward the standard abbreviations used in commercial patterns (e.g. 'knit 1' is written out instead of abbreviated as 'k1').'

Exploring Felting *Joan Fisher, Kangaroo Press, 1997*

This is one of the few Australian books on felting and Joan Fisher is considered a grande dame of felting. Instructions are included for 29 projects, for beginners and advanced-level felters.

reading

... she told him as she

... Menn... ...nued Hermux.
...a har... ...turn in the hall and rolled
... Hermu...
know about that?" she demanded.
...mon knowledge, Tucka," continued
... Mennu ...rching your youth for-
behind schedule. Budgets straining.
Etc. Etc...
... you thi... ...completely vicious liar.
...ta of truth in any of it. And if you repeat
to anyone I'll sue you for every pathetic

...erself. "Well enough of that!" she said
... to see you a... ...gas. She gave Hermux
..., threw her skates into reverse, and
...n the hall waving a languid farewell with
...ed claws.

Chapter 13

ON THE PAPER TRAIL

Hermux was too jangled to warm up his acorn casserole in
... oven. He stood with it next to the sink and ate a couple
... spoonfuls right out of the pan. Then he put it back in
... ...ogerator and opened a box of crackers. He wan-
... ...ack to his study munching slowly, pondering the
unsettling events of the day, and studying the package from
... Dandiffer that sat expectantly at the centre of his desk.
...erfle ruffled her wings noisily in her cage.
'Oh, gosh, Terfle!' said Hermux. 'I completely forgot

Having always survived by being street smart, as opposed to book smart, it wasn't until I read Jill Ker Conway's Australian autobiographies (*The Road from Coorain* and *True North: A Memoir*) that I could see the worth in combining the two. I read her vivid tales as a 25-year-old wondering what on earth I was going to do as a single mother with holes in my education. My scholastic success at the three high schools I went to was patchy, as I hadn't gone to university, or travelled. I came to realise I had little to work with to build a fabulous future.

Ker Conway's description of attending university despite her mother's lack of support was intoxicating and inspiring and led me to enrol as a mature age student in an English literature/journalism distance education degree at Melbourne's Monash University. Doing my degree by distance meant I didn't have to find daycare for two-year-old Monte. When, three years later, I was offered a freelance job to write a small weekly piece for *The Weekend Australian*'s book pages titled 'It Changed My Life', I jumped at the chance. Not only was it exactly the kind of work I wanted to be doing, but it also meant I had an excuse to ask other people about their own Jill-Ker-Conway moments.

Of the many actors, politicians, business leaders and authors to whom I put the question 'What was the book that changed your life?', the answers given by Pru Goward (sex discrimination commissioner), Sophie Cunningham (book publisher) and Mark Davis (author) were the most memorable because they reinforced why reading is so crucially linked to finding your way through life. In their stories they share how their place in the world, and the way they see themselves, shifted because of a book they read.

For Pru Goward, it was E.H. Carr's *What is History?* Reading his book after listening to an economics lecture at Adelaide University, Goward decided to become a journalist instead of her planned economics career.

'Like a lot of bright kids, I wandered through, getting all the answers right but never understanding what I was doing. *What is History?* confirmed that I couldn't be haphazard: sometimes moralistic and sometimes objective and rigorous. This style of thinking flowed over into personal relationships because it helped me understand the subject and the objective, and distance myself from what appeared to be overwhelming personal problems.'

Sophie Cunningham, a book publisher, says she is a little embarrassed the book that changed her life wasn't Proust but John Irving's *The World According to Garp*.

'I was 18, my parents were separating and my family was in chaos. I almost had an epiphany when I read the scene in *Garp* when the car hits the house and she bites off his penis. That scene triggered a profound sense of relief that life is absurd and so you can't control it: that it is normal for life to be out of control and I don't have to worry. I can laugh at it.'

When author Mark Davis read André Gide's *If It Dies* he understood life was not about how you lived it, rather what you thought of yourself along the way.

'Reading him made me realise my own life was possible. It seems strange to think that I held a book in my hands, a collection of pages with a cover, that changed the whole way I thought and the whole way I lived my life from then on.'

I love buying books and have never been able to bring myself to throw any away — even those the equivalent of a Michael Bolton CD — because each one says something about me: who I was when I bought it or what others must think of me to have chosen it as a gift. One of the first things Roberto and I did when we moved in together was build a floor-to-ceiling bookcase for our combined collection.

For a book to have a profound effect on you there has to be an alignment of factors. I have reread Jill Ker Conway's books but felt nothing like I did when I first read them ten years ago. It has to be the right book at the right time, though you need to read regularly for such brilliance to occur. From the time you are old enough to understand a story, books can affect you in many ways and it's never too early to put this in motion. I bought *The Little Engine That Could* for Lucy's fourth Christmas and Roberto took one look at it and said with a smile 'Of course you did', knowing all too well how important it is to me my children believe they can do anything. With the same purpose in mind I gave Monte Richard Bach's *Jonathan Livingston Seagull* a few years ago. I wanted to tell him, without being obvious or didactic, that he doesn't have to be like everyone else, that he can strive for his own dreams. I didn't say a lot when I gave it to him, just that I had really enjoyed it and thought he might too. I was interested to see if he would read the book for the story or read between the lines. He read between the lines. But he didn't make a big deal of it, just used Jonathan Livingston Seagull to draw an analogy once.

Reading offers more to kids than the possibility of a life-changing experience, and of course, at a young age, that's not what they are looking for. What they want, in fact, is probably the opposite: they want to know everyone else out there is just like them because that is way more comfortable than trailblazing. I read to Monte every night as he went to sleep and I still have the book that he first read by himself, *Sammy The Seal*. It is no literary masterpiece but I kept it because I will never forget the look on his face, nor the excitement I felt, when he first read those words all by himself. Perhaps his memory helped him, but he believed he was reading and — apart from walking and talking — I don't think there is any greater achievement for a small child.

Lucy has three stories read to her each night and it's a routine she cherishes. Roberto usually reads to her, a habit that started when she had an earlier bedtime and I was never certain what time I would get home from work. There is nothing I love more than to end the day lying with her on her bed reading wonderful stories about Olivia the pig or saying together 'Frank was a monster who wanted to dance. I know I could do it if they gave me a chance' (because you've read it so many times).

Of course there is no guarantee they will pick up the baton and run with it. Monte, once he had learnt to read, became a devoted reader. I bought him lots of first reader books and borrowed more from the library. And then reading became uncool. He just stopped, right at the age when he needed to read the most: nine years old. Nothing Roberto or I said sparked him to pick up the books that were sitting, decidedly unread, on his shelf. So I bought him a few novels based around his favourite subject, surfing. They excited him enough to keep them by his bed, but he wasn't so keen to read them.

A few months later I was in a bookstore looking for a Christmas present for Monte and saw *Time Stops for No Mouse: A Hermux Tantamoq Adventure* sitting on the counter. I picked it up and started reading the back when the shop assistant asked me how old was the child I was thinking of giving it to.

'Ten,' I answered.

She then looked at me with the sort of pursed mouth that goes with tilting your head from shoulder to shoulder. 'Obviously without knowing the child I can't really say either way but that book, well, it's a bit dark. I'm not sure if it's really a kid's book.'

'I'll take it.'

When Monte unwrapped it on Christmas day the dismal look on his face said 'Great, a book'. Ignoring him, I told of how the lady in the shop said I shouldn't buy it for him because maybe it would be too scary. That was half-interesting to him but it wasn't until we went to see its author, Michael Hoeye, speak at the Sydney Festival, that Monte got excited about reading again.

Hoeye was brilliant. He had the kids hanging off his every word as he explained why he had written the book — which was remarkable if our situation was typical, because it meant most had been made to go and listen to him. *Time Stops for No Mouse* started with an email from Hoeye to his wife who was away on business for a long period. The adventures of Hermux Tantamoq, the watch-making mouse, were meant to be a private story, delivered in daily instalments, to keep her amused. Instead they became an international best-seller.

So Monte picked up Hoeye's book and couldn't put it down. I read it after him and loved it, too. It's not dark, it's just not patronising — which is what a lot of children's books tend to be and why Monte avoids reading. So I set out to find books for him that spoke his language and found myself revisiting books I read as a child.

A.B. Facey's *A Fortunate Life* was one such book. I literally had to force Monte to read it and, just as I thought, it turned out to be another 'Fly Away Home'. That's an expression we use for 'I-know-you-are-going-to-like-it-so-just-try-it'. It was born years ago after I dragged Monte to a movie he said he didn't want to see called 'Fly Away Home', which became his all-time favourite movie — for a minute, anyway.

Now *A Fortunate Life* is his second favourite book after Hoeye's. Next I bought *The Secret Diary of Adrian Mole, aged 13¾*. After he told me reading is boring, I told Monte he had to read the first chapter and if he didn't like it he didn't have to read further. Reading it he had something close to an epiphany. He couldn't believe I had given him a book that talked about sex and pimples and how annoying parents are. He loved it. Now he's 11 I really want him to read *Lord of the Flies* (I am keen to ask him which character he identifies with).

Lucy is a read-to-me-oholic but a tough negotiator when it comes to choosing books. She has steadfast favourites and while I know it's important to read the same book over and over, it can get boring for the reader. So as Monte did, I thought she, too, needed a little shocking to get her tasting something different.

I found Roald Dahl's *Revolting Rhymes* in a secondhand bookstore and I will never forget the look on her face when I read it for the first time. She loves fairytales and couldn't believe what was coming out of my mouth. It was sacrilegious. Dahl scandalously pilloried each one of her beloved fairytales. At first she couldn't work out why I insisted on reading the wrong words to such familiar stories but then she worked out what was going on. A conspiratorial look of glee came over her face and she practically stopped breathing so as not to miss one naughty word. And that is what books are all about — being naughty, pushing boundaries, they whisper to you what you are secretly thinking but couldn't possibly say out loud. If your children believe that is what books have hiding between their covers, buried amongst all those words, then I can only suggest you build yourself a bookcase.

books to read

I keep a list of books I want to buy. Some are for me and some are books I want to get for the kids or Roberto. I keep a list because I all too often forget what I want to buy or borrow after being told by a friend of a must-read, or reading book reviews in the newspaper. It's daunting walking into a bookstore or library and trying to unearth the perfect read – it's much better going in armed with your selection. So for that reason I hope these lists help you.

on books and reading

Reading Magic *Mem Fox, illustrated by Judy Horacek*

It's never too soon to read aloud to your child. Stories are magical. Let's share the magic, Fox says. This is a highly motivational book, citing examples of success by reading to the very young.

Boys and Books *James Moloney*

Boys become book-shy when they reach adolescence, which is a great shame because this is when they most need a helping hand from someone other than their parents. Moloney takes a broad look at why this happens and offers a great reading list.

Babies Need Books *Dorothy Butler*

This is an excellent reference book, focusing on the pre-school years and offering a wealth of suggested reading. First published in 1980, the selection is so good that nearly all of Butler's recommendations are still in print.

Chushla and Her Books *Dorothy Butler*

> The fascinating story of the role of books in the life of a handicapped child as written by her grandmother, Dorothy Butler, who was awarded a Diploma of Education for this three-year study.

Don't Leave Childhood Without *Specialist Children's Booksellers (SCB)*

> The SCB is a group of specialist children's booksellers in NSW who have selected what they believe are the best books for babies through to young adults. This booklet is well worth a place on your bookshelf and can be bought from good children's bookshops.

babies 0 to 1 year

Babies need to enjoy conversations with their parents and grandparents, and not be taught things in a formal way. They learn from looking at faces, not being told things. If you teach children in a formal way at this age, they tend to learn things through rote, not through understanding.

> Sebastian Kraemer,
> co-author of Britain's Royal College of Paediatrics
> and Child Health report, *Helpful Parenting*.

I Went Walking *Sue Machin*

> Babies love repetitive text, being asked questions, and soft illustrations, which is exactly what this farmyard stroll offers.

My Home *Lothian*

These Australian board books are filled with photographs of everyday items that your child comes into contact with, from a spoon to the clothesline. They are spellbinding because the photographs allow the recognition to be instantaneous. They are also perfect for returning to when your child begins to learn to read.

Peepo! *Janet and Allan Ahlberg*

Is what we see all there is to see? The clever devices on each page show how babies take in the world around them. Each picture initially shows the most obvious focus for attention, shown through the small peephole, but turn the page and that's when discoveries are made.

Letters; Opposites; Numbers; Colours *John Burningham*

With his beautiful pastel pencil drawings, Burningham softens the obvious educational focus of his warm and inviting series.

Where, Oh Where, Is Baby Bear *Debi Gliori*

Daddy Bear is outside looking for Baby Bear, and you help by peeking under the flaps. It's a warm and comforting story, and the pictures are full of bewitching details that require lots of visits.

Brown Bear, Brown Bear, What Do You See? *Bill Martin Jnr, illustrated by Eric Carle*

Considered a long-time favourite among the very young, perhaps because it cleverly combines repetition and the absurd (key ingredients for any children's book) while also showing how to open your eyes to the world around you.

Fuzzy Yellow Ducklings *Mathew Van Fleet*

> By combining different learning concepts in a simple format, babies will associate counting with lots of fun.

Miffy *Dick Bruna*

> The Miffy series will be treasured long after they have done their work. You and your child may well remember them as their first real books.

toddlers 1 to 3 years

When we take the time to read aloud to the children in our lives, we bond closely with them in a secret society associated with the books we've shared. The fire of literacy is created by the emotional sparks that fly when a child, a book, and the person reading make contact. It isn't achieved by the book alone, nor by the adult who's reading aloud — it's the relationship winding among all three, bringing them together in easy harmony.

> Mem Fox, *Reading Magic*

Between two and four (years old) the world opens up to the child. Whereas before this time her curiosity was confined to her actual surroundings, she now wants, increasingly, to go out into the world, to learn about everything, to become involved.

> Dorothy Butler, *Babies Need Books*

Rosie's Walk *Pat Hutchins*

Rosie the hen goes on a walk, never noticing the fox-shaped shadow behind her. Classically simple, most of this story is played out in the illustrations. Dorothy Butler, in *Babies Need Books*, suggests you read this book to your two-year-old without mentioning the fox, as his hungry pursuit, dogged by a series of catastrophes relating to Rosie's walk, is expressed only through the pictures. Wait until the child you are reading to works it out for themselves and watch the wonder come across their face as they do.

The Very Hungry Caterpillar *Eric Carle*

A must for every toddler. In this perfect picture book, our famished friend eats his way through the ingeniously layered pages, introducing a number of early concepts.

Dear Zoo *Rod Campbell*

Many strange packages are sent from the zoo before the perfect pet arrives. A lift-the-flap favourite.

Ten in the Bed *Penny Dale*

Just when does cosy become crowded? A subtle variation on the traditional rhyme gives the familiar a little more character.

Wheels on the Bus *Paul Zelinsky*

I wish we had bought two copies of this because we have nearly destroyed the one we have with too much love and affection. Delightfully detailed, the humorous illustrations and dozens of flaps to lift, tabs to pull and wheels to turn, bring this traditional song to life.

Where's Spot *Eric Hill*

> Every child falls in love with Spot who is clever at counting, naming colours, going to parties, playing hide-and-seek, and lots of other things your child will identify with.

Harry the Dirty Dog *Gene Zion*

> With only two colours, Harry could be left gathering dust on the shelf if it were not for its literary excellence. A white dog with black spots, Harry, when left to his own devices, becomes a black dog with white spots. Isn't this just how your child loves to spend their day? (First published 1956)

preschoolers 3 to 5 years

The importance of well-chosen picture books for children in these formative years when they are brimming with curiosity and wonder cannot be stressed enough. As young children begin to grasp the relationship between text and the spoken word, they will be captivated by strong rhythm and rhyme, themes to which they can relate and a wide range of illustrations which both excite their interest and engage their imagination.

Specialist Children's Booksellers, NSW.

Frank Was a Monster Who Wanted to Dance *Keith Graves*

> We bought this for Lucy and Monte while on holidays in the United States. Graves draws the most delightful monster —

in both an illustrative and a literary sense — who wanted to dance and knew he could boogie if they gave him a chance. It didn't take long before both kids could remember the lines off by heart, but it is the last two pages that makes Graves' work a must-have.

Olivia *Ian Falconer*

Olivia is the new pig on the block of children's literature and well worth inviting into your home. She's feisty, independent and great at negotiating numerous bedtime stories. Olivia loves dressing up, singing songs, building sandcastles, dancing, painting on walls and sleeping (maybe).

Guess How Much I Love You *Sam McBratney*

Sometimes, when you love someone very much you want to find a way of describing how great your feelings are. But as little nutbrown hare and big nutbrown hare discover, love is not an easy thing to measure.

Where the Wild Things Are *Maurice Sendak*

The best picture books have many layers. This story about Max and 'the wild things' explores a young child's search for independence and growth, the importance of imagination and the unconditional love of a parent.

The Story about Ping *Majorie Flack, illustrated by Kurt Weise*

This realistic animal story has been an abiding favourite for generations. Weise's illustrations capture the spirit of this lively tale of a rebellious little duck who lives on a 'wise-eyed boat' on the Yangtze River. (First published in 1933.)

Gordon's Got a Snookie *Lisa Shanahan, illustrated by Wayne Harris*

> I bought this, a brilliantly illustrated and funny tale, for Lucy because, like Gordon the gorilla, she, too, has a snookie, except hers is called 'bishy'. I can't tell you how many people have asked me why I haven't taken her security blanket away. Snookies or bishies are relinquished when the child is feeling empowered, not disrespected.

The Deep *Tim Winton, illustrated by Karen Louise*

> Without Winton's thoughtfully-written book about Alice's fears about swimming in the deep, where her family play every day, and Louise's true-to-life pictures, convincing our Lucy that swimming was fun, not scary, would have been much harder.

We're Going on a Bear Hunt *Michael Rosen, illustrated by Helen Oxenbury*

> This is ideal for young children to read along with and join in all the wonderful noises and actions. They'll love it.

Hairy Maclary From Donaldson's Dairy *Lynley Dodd*

> All Hairy Maclary's friends have names as wonderful as his which makes this book a treat to read aloud to your child — and soon they will be 'reading' it to you. What a confidence builder that is.

The Little Engine That Could *Watty Piper*

> This famous story, first told in 1930, about the little engine who got to the top of the mountain all because he kept telling him-self: I think I can — I think I can — I think I can.

infants school 5 to 7 years

Ownership of books means an ownership of reading. If you haven't already begun to build your children their own library, then now is the time to start. Good books can survive all ages and stages and are well worth collecting.

Green Eggs and Ham; The Cat in the Hat; The Cat in the Hat Comes Back; The Sneetches and Other Stories
> And, of course, all the other addictive and delightful works by Dr Seuss that are fun, phonetic and unforgettable. Dr Seuss's treasures are the perfect books to start with when children are ready to learn to read.

Revolting Rhymes *Roald Dahl*
> Roald Dahl gives us his famous satirical spin on six traditional tales including 'Snow White' ('From now on, Queen, you're Number Two. Snow White is prettier than you!' says the Magic Mirror) and 'The Three Little Pigs'. This one stopped our kids dead in their tracks because they were so surprised at its naughtiness. They love it.

Rose Meets Mr Wintergarten *Bob Graham*
> Mr Wintergarten is scary. His garden is grey and sunless and it's guarded, they say. Rose Summers lives next door and her garden is a playground of happiness and flowers. So what happens when young Rose loses her ball in old Mr Wintergarten's garden?

The Iron Man *Ted Hughes*

> Ted Hughes, recent poet laureate of Britain, wrote this compelling tall tale in 1968. Clearly, the need for its message of peace has not diminished in the decades since. Simple, repetitive sentences carry the mesmerising spirit of traditional fairy tales.

Wilfred Gordon McDonald Partridge *Mem Fox, illustrated by Julie Vivas*

> A touching and beautifully illustrated story about childhood, old age and the importance of precious memories.

A Fish Out of Water *Helen Palmer, illustrated by P.D. Eastman*

> A small boy tells his tale at record speed of how he was warned by the pet shop owner not to overfeed his new fish. Of course he does. But when the local pool, police and fire brigade can't solve the problem of housing his now gigantic gold fish, who can? One smart little fish-owning boy, that's who. Over 25 years old but without the slightest hint of age.

Alexander and the Terrible, Horrible, No Good, Very Bad Day *Judith Viorst, illustrated by Ray Cruz*

> Everybody knows the feeling of a day when absolutely nothing goes right and the chaos and calamity in Alexander's day will be familiar to young and old.

The Velveteen Rabbit *Margery Williams, illustrated by Michael Hague*

> A sentimental classic first published in 1922, it is perfect for any child who's ever thought that maybe, just maybe, his or her toys have feelings.

primary school 7 to 10 years

The more that you read, the more things that you will know. The more that you learn the more places you will go.

Dr Seuss

Children of this age will seesaw between wanting to practise reading aloud and having you read to them. These books are perfect for either occasion.

Selby's Secret; Selby Snaps; Selby Snowbound *Duncan Ball, illustrated by Allan Stoman*

> This collection of the crazy misadventures of the only talking dog in Australia begins with *Selby's Secret*, in which this pooch has to keep his special powers quiet. How hard is that going to be? Monte devoured the whole series.

The Magnificent Noise and Other Marvels *Anna Fienberg, illustrated by Kim Gamble*

> Monte was given this book for his birthday and he fell in love with the wonderfully original and off-beat stories in which five children show their particular talents. While each is a stand-alone tale, a spider cleverly links the stories. We are reading it to Lucy and she is spellbound.

Stuart Little *E.B. White*

> If your children enjoyed the movie, then they will love the book. Written by the author of that other perennial favourite, *Charlotte's Web*.

Tashi *Anna & Barbara Fienberg, illustrated by Kim Gamble*

    Tashi has come from far away on the back of a swan to delight children with his adventures in a series of 'chapter books'. This Australian series was a favourite of Monte as he was learning to read.

Jonathan Livingstone Seagull *Richard Bach*

    I have not come across this on any reading list but believe it should be on everyone's. Written in the early 1970s, it has become a phenomenon. I gave it to Monte to read after we watched Robin Williams' brilliant performance in *Dead Poet's Society*. It is an inspirational book and while a primary-school child may not uncover every one of its layers, it will certainly speak to them about how important it is to follow your own path.

Time Stops for No Mouse *Michael Hoeye*

    This is not a difficult book for a child to read alone, except for the character's names. Hoeye said he created their fanciful monikers from jumbling letters, so no wonder they are often hard to pronounce. It's a little dark in places, but then so is life. If you are not sure whether your child is ready for Hermux Tantamoq, the clever mouse who is a watchmaker and mystery solver, read it aloud to them — but be warned, you may well find you take it to bed yourself, too.

The Harry Potter Series *J.K. Rowling*

    Do I need to explain why? I don't think so, because if your child hasn't read a book from this series, had one read to them, or seen the movie, then you clearly need to get out more.

Tales of a Fourth Grade Nothing *Judy Blume*

I was a huge Judy Blume fan when I was in primary school. Her made-for-troubled-adolescents text got me over many hurdles and through lots of uncomfortable situations. She still has currency because she knows exactly how to speak to those who need to hear her most.

Storm Boy *Colin Thiele*

Who can forget Mr Percival and the beautiful relationship he had with the boy they call Storm Boy? It's a sad book but then, as the back cover says, everyone knows that birds like Mr Percival never really die. A classic Australian children's book first published in 1966 and well worth revisiting.

Aesop's Fables

I pull this one out when I am having trouble explaining right from wrong. A neatly-woven tale can often do the job a lot better than me. *Aesop's Fables* may seem old-fashioned but there is often no better allegory than 'The Crow and Raven' when you want to show your child that they will always be rewarded for being themselves rather than something they are not.

adolescence

It is my belief that there are no 'parents' aids' which can compare with the book in its capacity to establish and maintain a relationship with a child. Its effects extend far beyond the covers of the actual book, and invade every

aspect of life. **Parents and children who share books come to share the same frame of reference ... And books can play a major part in this process. Because by their very nature they are rooted in language, and because language is essential to human communication, and communication is the life blood of relationships, books matter.**

Dorothy Butler, *Babies Need Books*

A Fortunate Life *A.B. Facey*

Despite a brutal early life, service in World War I and a hard existence of constant toil, Facey tells his story with humility and the certainty that he did, indeed, lead a fortunate life. A motivating tale written in a boy's-own style but just as appealing for girls, too.

The Diary of Anne Frank *Anne Frank*

The secret journal of a Dutch Jewish girl written during the time her family was in hiding from the Nazis during World War II. It is a heart-rending account of what it is like to spend your youth in such desperate circumstances.

Catcher in the Rye *J.D. Salinger*

Salinger's only novel, this is a rambling monologue by 17-year-old Holden Caulfield. He runs away from boarding school and, drifting through New York, shares with us his wry, cynical observations. He is fighting against having to become an adult, which he sees as a form of surrender, and doesn't know whether to go home or wander the streets.

Two Weeks with the Queen *Morris Gleitzman*

With humour as his licence, Gleitzman takes an interesting
and unconventional approach to tackling death, AIDS and
homosexuality. Colin Mudford's parents send him to stay with
relatives in London because his brother is dying of cancer. But
rather than close his eyes to what is happening to his family,
Colin reaches deep within and surprises everyone.

The Number Devil: A Mathematical Adventure *Hans Magnus
Enzensberger, illustrated by Rotraut Susanne Berner*

We bought this for Monte because he wasn't enjoying, nor
understanding, why he was doing maths. This is a magical tale
about 12-year-old Robert who hates his maths teacher (haven't
we all been Robert at one time or another?). One night, in a
dream, he meets the Number Devil who knows how to make
maths devilishly simple and so brings a complex and difficult
subject to life. Note to parents who don't like maths: well worth
reading yourself.

To Kill a Mockingbird *Harper Lee*

This is a story of justice. But justice is often a difficult concept
for young people to grasp because it is never black and white.
Which is why teenagers should read it — but when? It will
probably make them ask you lots of questions that are hard to
answer, but if you believe your child is ready for such a
worthwhile, though difficult, life lesson then buy them their
own copy to keep forever. Otherwise, wait a couple of years. But
make sure they read it before they reach adulthood.

Freaky Friday *Mary Rodgers*

A light and funny book about a 13-year-old girl who gains a sympathetic understanding of her relationship with her mother, and of her mother's life, when the two switch bodies.

The Getting of Wisdom *H.H. Richardson*

A gifted, unhappy adolescent in a late nineteenth-century Australian boarding school uses a love of the arts as an escape from the oppressive narrowness of the school regime.

My Brilliant Career *Miles Franklin*

Sybylla Melvyn, growing up in late nineteenth-century Australia, refuses to conform. Rather, she learns about life, the arts and love on an outback farm and in the city.

The Secret Diary of Adrian Mole, aged 13¾ *Sue Townsend*

In his secret diary, British teen Adrian Mole excruciatingly details every morsel of his turbulent adolescence. Mixed in with daily reports about the zit sprouting on his chin are heart-rending passages about his parents' chaotic marriage. Adrian's angst is timeless.

The Little Prince *Antoine de Saint-Exupéry*

The narrator of this gorgeous parable is an air pilot who tells how, having made a forced landing in the Sahara Desert, he meets a little prince. The wise and enchanting stories the prince tells about the planet where he lives with three volcanoes and a haughty flower, about the other planets and their rulers, and about his fight with the bad seeds, make him an entrancing and unforgettable character.

classics

What makes a classic? This list is a combination of factors; standing the test of time, common themes, overcoming adversity, growing up, friendship and discovery. The most obvious I have left to last: they are all still available.

Little Women *Louisa M. Alcott*
Alice in Wonderland *Lewis Carroll*
The Wonderful World of Oz *L. Frank Baum*
Charlie and the Chocolate Factory *Roald Dahl*
Wind in the Willows *Kenneth Grahame*
The Lion the Witch and the Wardrobe *C.S. Lewis*
The Magic Pudding *Norman Lindsay*
The Story of Doctor Doolittle *Hugh Lofting*
The Railway Children *E. Nesbit*
The Borrowers *Mary Norton*
The Tale of Peter Rabbit *Beatrix Potter*
Swallows and Amazons *Arthur Ransome*
Charlotte's Web *E.B. White*
Lord of the Flies *William Golding*
The Adventures of Tom Sawyer *Mark Twain*
David Copperfield *Charles Dickens*